praise for
FROM MY FRONT ROW SEAT BY SUSAN BINKLEY

I cried. I laughed out loud. And I thought about faith with fresh eyes while reading the heart-rending stories that Susan Binkley tells so very well. This book is a hard look into the face of evil. Even more, it is a hope-filled encounter with the power of God.

STEVE BRALLIER
Promoter, agent, and author of *Mitka's Secret: A True Story of Child Slavery and Surviving the Holocaust*

Even when the stories she's telling about the women and children she's known at Blue Monarch are hard to hear, Susan Binkley's honest, humorous, and humble voice compels us to listen. Like George Gershwin's symphony "Rhapsody in Blue," which Susan alludes to halfway through the book, her stories move gracefully from harmony to disharmony and back in a captivating rhythm, concluding in a crescendo of hope and healing. *From My Front Row Seat: A Collection of Stories from My Time Working Alongside Women in Recovery* mixes pain and humor, pragmatism and humility, into the strong faith that underlies every word. This book will transform anyone who reads it into a believer in miracles.

VIRGINIA CRAIGHILL
Professor Emerita of English at The University of the South

From My Front Row Seat will take you on an incredible journey, which I am sure you will never forget. Almost twenty years ago it was my good fortune for Susan to share with me her dream, which she believed was a call from God. She responded to that call by launching a program that has served almost one thousand women and children. Following the Blue Monarch journey for these many years has truly been a transformative experience for me and for my family. I will always be grateful. This is a book that you will have trouble putting down once you have started and I predict you will be grateful for the experience.

HOWELL ADAMS
Blue Monarch founding benefactor

I have had the privilege and joy of seeing Susan grow from a child to who she is today. It is rare that a person gets to actually live out her dream and then speak or write about it with a completely open heart. Susan shares her marvelous journey that has blessed her and many others, but because she is a good listener, she is also able to share the journeys of others. It is simply amazing what the Lord can do when you let Him lead, and to write about it as Susan has done.

PAUL WALKER
Business owner/investor

Perhaps the most beautiful testimonial we have ever known. Susan's book presents a multilayered story of someone being called by God to undertake a mission for which she seemingly had no competence or even interest—and ultimately, by what can only be attributed to God's design, has developed a remarkably successful and life-changing program for *permanent* alcohol and drug addiction recovery. Susan's willingness to share her innermost thoughts, including her perceived limitations and how she struggled at first to allow God to lead and equip her, affords a sincere testimony to what can be accomplished when we center our lives on God's will, not ours.

SCOTT AND GAIL MATTHEWS
Blue Monarch supporters

My respect and love for Susan are anchored in her transparency, her love, and her truthfulness in her obedient faith journey. In reading Susan's book, laughing, crying, worshiping, and learning were center stage. Observing the ministry of Blue Monarch, as it grew and excelled in serving the women and their children, exceeded the blessing I expected. Reading of the wisdom/knowing what to do, the knowledge/knowing how to do, and the discernment/knowing when to do, so beautifully ministering to each circumstance, was one inspiration after another. All acts of service exalted the faithfulness, steadfastness, and love of our Savior. I invite you to pull up a front row seat, receive manna for your soul and living water to refresh your spirit as you soar on the fragile yet powerful wings of Blue Monarch. Read and receive His blessing!

JANICE BOWLING
Tennessee State Senator

You are going to love the view *From My Front Row Seat* because Susan Binkley communicates in a compelling, "I can't put this book down" manner. Her stories evoke more than sympathy; they demand a response and produce a tenacious desire to do something to help someone who cannot repay you. This book will encourage you and change you for the better.

KEN ABRAHAM
New York Times bestselling author

from my FRONT ROW SEAT

A COLLECTION OF STORIES FROM MY TIME WORKING ALONGSIDE WOMEN IN RECOVERY

Susan Binkley

Fedd Books
P.O. Box 341973
Austin, TX 78734
www.thefeddagency.com

Published in association with The Fedd Agency, Inc., a literary agency.

ISBN: 978-1-957616-28-5
eISBN: 978-1-957616-29-2
LCCN: 2022923343

Cover design by Mackenna Cotten
Cover photo and author photo by Dona Masters Photography

Printed in the United States of America

This book is dedicated to the courageous women and children of Blue Monarch, who impress and inspire me every single day. Thank you for allowing me to share your remarkable journeys.

Now glory be to God, who by his mighty power at work within us is able to do far more than we would ever dare to ask or even dream of—infinitely beyond our highest prayers, desires, thoughts, or hopes. (Ephesians 3:20 TLB)

TABLE OF CONTENTS

part three

FOREWORD

by Jeannie Driver Campbell

When I received the phone call from Susan asking if I would write the foreword for this book, my response was, "Absolutely I will," followed by a rush of emotion that brought tears to my eyes. I am completely honored to be a part of this amazing story. The author, Susan Binkley, is a fierce protector, an excellent leader, an out-of-the-box thinker. She is genuine to the core and one of the funniest people I know. So get ready to laugh and cry at the same time.

I have known Susan for nineteen years, and I am forever grateful for all that she has added to my life. She has loved me when I was unlovable, believed in me when I felt there was nothing in me to believe in, and challenged me to reach for greatness in all that I do. She has stood by me in my greatest times as well as my darkest days.

In 2003, I sat in front of Susan for the first time. I was a broken mess, trapped in the vicious cycle of addiction and incarceration. I had three young daughters and was almost completely hopeless. Susan was interviewing me for a potential spot in her new residential recovery program called Blue Monarch. She greeted me as a beacon of hope and exuded a compassion that I hadn't felt in a very long time. Almost immediately, I felt a connection with her.

My daughters and I were accepted into Blue Monarch, and that night we laid our heads down in the safety and comfort of our new home, together for the first time in a long while. I watched Susan come in day in and day out with a heart to serve. She was always ready to tackle any challenge that came up, and she taught us to do the same. She was fighting for the underdog. She believed that God could heal addiction just like he could heal anything else. And because she believed it, we did too!

I wish I could say that I completed the program, but after six months, I thought I was ready, and my daughters and I left Blue Monarch. Susan was heartbroken, to say the least, because she knew it was a mistake. With tears in her eyes, she tried to convince me to stay—but I had made up my mind. Within four months after leaving Blue Monarch, I had four federal indictments and was on my way to prison. Susan visited me in the county jail while I waited to be moved to federal prison. She never gave up on me, and I was always strengthened by her visits.

After being in prison for a couple of years, I was transferred across several states to another prison. My brother was allowed to transport me. Susan surprised me by meeting us at a Waffle House restaurant in the middle of the night when we passed through Tennessee. Once again, she had not given up on me.

My sentence was reduced from six to four years, and after my release, I contacted Susan. She allowed me to volunteer at Blue Monarch teaching Bible studies. She *still* believed in me! It was such a blessing to return to where my healing began. After I'd been a volunteer for three years, Susan felt she needed someone with my experience on the staff and offered me a full-time position, where I have been for the last eight years. I now have the honor of serving on the Blue Monarch Leadership Team as the program director.

Susan has not only touched the lives of my children and me, but God has used her in the healing process of hundreds of other families as well. As you read this book, you will be diving into her firsthand experience with the depths of despair that go hand in hand with the brokenness of addiction, mixed with God's amazing mountaintops of miracles. I pray God fills you with hope and much laughter as you journey through one of the greatest books you'll ever read!

PREFACE

For reasons I don't really understand, I wanted to grow up to have multiple husbands, like Elizabeth Taylor. She recycled one, which made little sense, but I found the variety quite fascinating. I also wanted to be a country music singer and an astronaut, whichever came first. What I did not want to be was a missionary—and I was quite certain about that.

Missionaries and their families occasionally visited the small Southern Baptist church where I grew up, and I always felt sorry for them. They looked tired and weary, they rarely laughed, and without fail, they wore clothes that were clearly out of style by about five years. I always imagined if truly given a choice, they would not go back to the mission field. My plan was to avoid eye contact with God so he wouldn't notice me and send me to Africa, but I was hopeful he would still consider me for a spot in heaven. It was a tricky balance.

Me as a fourth grader in my blue glasses with bows

So here's how that turned out. In the fourth grade my best friend, Debbie, finally broke it to me that I couldn't sing. Okay, it was painful letting go, but I trusted her and gave up that fantasy cold turkey. Through the years I discovered I was exceptionally bad at math, and apparently this was sort of critical for an astronaut.

I did, however, chip away at my Elizabeth Taylor goal, and right after I married my third husband, God gave me a powerful dream one night that ultimately put me on a path to be a missionary of sorts. Turns out God found me even without the eye contact. Yup. I got the thing I tried so hard to avoid: the dreaded "call."

However, it didn't land me in Africa. It took me to my own backyard, where I have had a front row seat ever since—at the greatest show on earth. From where I sit, I get to see miracles so up close and personal, I can reach out and touch them. They take my breath away at least a few times a week. But from the same seat, I may also get my heart broken into a million pieces—and both can happen on the same day.

In looking back, I have a whole new perspective on the hardworking missionaries I saw as a child. I no longer think they were weary. They were probably carrying the hard-core memories of the suffering they had seen and heard, which were impossible to unsee and unhear. They may not have laughed much because their hearts were left behind with the people they served. And the outdated clothes? Well, I've got nothing for that one. But I understand, now, why they always went back. Yeah, that one I totally get.

part one

"WHAT MADE YOU WANT TO DO THIS?"

"What made you want to open a residential recovery program for women and their children?"

I've heard this question more times than I can count. It's funny the way it's worded, because it implies that something would have to *make* me start Blue Monarch—that I couldn't possibly want something like this on my own. Well, in looking back, I suppose that is pretty much what happened. Someone did make me want it.

It all started with a dream back in 1995. I had just married my third husband, Clay, and we were basically strangers. In fact, we were married for almost a year before I discovered he could play the guitar. We never knew each other in school but met at our twenty-year high school reunion, where he won the "Most Eligible Bachelor" award, and I won "Most Interesting Pet." (I had rescued a zebra from a small neighborhood pen.) After dating for only three months, we decided to get married, but since we thought it would make us look crazy, we agreed to wait one more month. Four sounded so much better than three.

It was a surprise wedding. We invited both families to my house for Thanksgiving and had the preacher show up and marry us on the spot while we had our families together. There is an old VHS video that shows the wide range of reactions. My mother began crying when we asked everyone to gather in one room. I'm not sure what she was expecting, but I guess she assumed it was big, or maybe she was thinking, *Not again*.

Clay's mother, on the other hand, bounced across the coffee table with bubbling excitement because Clay was nearly forty years old and had never been married. My father smirked as if to say, "You've outdone yourself this time." Everyone else landed somewhere between amused and appalled.

Oh, and to make things even stranger, the flower girl was Daisy, a deer my daughter and I raised from a baby. My eleven-year-old approved of the marriage, which was the most important requirement. In fact, after suffering with me through a few miserable boyfriends after her father and I divorced, she met Clay and said, "I want him living here by Christmas." That was the only endorsement I needed. The child had the best discernment of anyone I knew.

It is a mystery why God chose this particular timing, but one night shortly after Clay and I were married, I had a really powerful dream. Even as I was dreaming, I knew it was no ordinary dream and I needed to pay attention.

In the dream, I was seated at a massive table that looked like marble. Mine was the only chair, but I was aware there were three large figures standing behind me surrounded by extremely bright light, so brilliant I didn't even try to see their faces.

A thick book was placed in front of me that looked like it might weigh ten pounds. Somehow, I felt I was required to read it, even though I briefly resisted. It was so long! But then I understood it was something I really needed to do, so I opened the cover and got started.

The book explained in great detail how one might create and develop a long-term, residential recovery program for women and their children. It even described how the women would earn an income by producing a product. The volumes were filled with pages and pages of details, images, concepts, and answers to potential problems.

My dream ended as soon as I closed the back cover on the massive book. The next morning, I made jokes about how I had intercepted someone else's dream, because it had nothing to do with my life. I was a visual artist by trade and ran a horse farm with a small vacation rental. In addition to that, the book was all about helping women and children, and I did not particularly care for either.

I avoided joining groups of women, and when I couldn't, I removed myself as quickly as possible. I typically felt I had nothing in common with any female group, no matter who they were. Children were equally irritating, and from what I could tell, they also carried incredibly contagious germs, evidenced by the chronic runny nose on every child's face. My one child was the only one I liked. Obviously, the dream was intended for someone who cared about people more than I did. However, I told my husband and daughter about the strange dream and from then on referred to it as "that powerful dream."

After a couple of years, we decided to move. Even though I cherished my years at Xanadu Farm in Triune, Tennessee, I was eager to build a place that would feel like it belonged to Clay too. He embraced my horse-farm world. In fact, Clay was a bull rider back in his rodeo days, which made him fit right in, but we were all excited about a totally new adventure.

These were the criteria for our new home: I wanted a fantastic view, Clay wanted to hear water, and we all wanted a good school for my daughter. This search landed us on a bluff near a waterfall on the Cumberland Plateau, where we amazingly found all three. My horse farm had taken me away from a former art career, so with this move I looked forward to selling my work at a prestigious Nashville gallery that had represented me in the past.

The first time we drove through Tracy City on the way to the land we would ultimately purchase, I couldn't believe my eyes. The Grundy County high school building absolutely took my breath away. "Remember that powerful dream I had? That building was in my dream! How strange." I was not sure how to interpret that. Why was that building in my dream? I remembered it so clearly. I even recalled how the windows in the dream looked dark, as if the lights were off inside.

Shortly after we moved, the high school relocated to a new facility, which left the massive redbrick building vacant. *Oh no.* What did this mean? It made me a little nervous.

I finally decided perhaps I was to be a messenger to let someone know they could use that building to do what was described in my dream. I called people all across the country to deliver the exciting news, and no one cared. No one. I even walked through the empty school a few times, just to see if something struck me. I was still puzzled. Why was I so drawn to this building?

In the meantime, Clay and I purchased a small commercial building in the university town of Sewanee, Tennessee. Our plan was to renovate the charming space and then rent it out. A new friend came to me with a proposal. She loved to bake and wanted to open a bakery. As an artist, I thought it would be a fun project to design the concept, the logo, and the interior, but let her run it. In other words, I would do the fun part and she would do the hard part. I felt it also needed to be a coffee shop, so the partnership began. But I made it clear from the beginning: "I will not make even one coffee drink."

So The Blue Chair in Sewanee was born on the Fourth of July in 2000 and quickly became a popular gathering place for locals and students. It was a funky little spot with lots of personality and character. There was a fish tank inside a 1960s television and a cozy sitting area with a side table made from an old coffee grinder. (I sold this business in 2012 to a nice couple who saved my life, Jimmy and Sarah, and am no longer responsible for the amount of onion in the chicken salad or that half the place is now a tavern—just so you know.)

Unfortunately, after only four months my partner decided to go back into real estate, and overnight, I found myself in the food business. The day she walked out the back door, I stood in the kitchen looking at the massive Blodgett oven, realizing I did not even know how to turn it on. The room began to spin in slow motion, just like in the movies. I could barely breathe.

This outcome could not have been more outrageous. I did not know how to cook, nor how to bake even one thing. At family gatherings, I was the one designated to bring bags of chips and ice. In fact, I had just recently forgotten to remove the cardboard round before baking a frozen pizza and had cooked a roast with the white plastic quilt still attached to the bottom. And now I had a coffee shop and bakery and was about to feed innocent strangers. I immediately ran down to the local Piggly Wiggly, bought every cinnamon roll I could find for the next morning, and just prayed no one would notice the difference.

Too stubborn to give up, I decided to learn the food business and get through this crisis, with no clear plan on the other side. I hired people who did know how to cook and immediately dove into a sixty-to-seventy-hour workweek, just figuring it out as I went. I knew absolutely nothing about running this type of business, and in looking back, it is a wonder it survived at all. For instance, it never occurred to me to run reports of any kind, which was a nightmare for the accountant, and I didn't make bank deposits unless the register was so full of cash, I couldn't shut the drawer. There was a lot to learn. A whole lot.

There were days when I locked the door behind the last customer and literally collapsed onto the dirty hardwood floor, closed my eyes, spread my arms and legs as if I was making a snow angel, and enjoyed just a few minutes of feeling sorry for myself before cleaning up the mess to start all over again the next day. No doubt there are many restaurant owners who can relate. There was a day I drove home crying and frustrated with God, because this was clearly his fault. "Why did you let me take the wrong fork in the road?! Is this the best you can do with the gifts you've given me?" (Warning: You'd better watch out when you start challenging God like that.)

Despite my lack of passion for the food business, my little bakery and coffee shop thrived. It somehow became successful and developed into a popular destination for folks as my personal interest in the business also grew. It became important to me to provide an atmosphere that people enjoyed, and it turned into a fun creative outlet. A friend of mine said, "You used to create three-dimensional artwork with people inside, but now you have created an actual building with real people inside." We expanded our menu until we turned into more of a café, and sales steadily grew. I became one of those entrepreneurs who knew the townsfolk not by their names but by what they ate and drank, and I often found myself listening to personal problems as if I were a bartender. (A few of them I could have done without.)

Through this business, however, I was introduced to a world I never knew existed. Women came to me for employment, but they were not able to keep their jobs for long because of all the dreadful circumstances at home. Several women came to work embarrassed about their black eyes. One woman had a jealous husband who sat in the corner glaring at her until I had to ask him to leave. Two women told the same but separate and unrelated stories of being abandoned in the woods barefoot with no way out. And another described how she had been trapped in her house with the doors and windows nailed shut.

The hopelessness was overwhelming, and I could only imagine how the environment and dysfunction affected their children. What were they going through while all this was happening around them? Were the children abused as well? At the time, I was completely naïve about the huge role addiction played in all the chaos. On my way to and from work, I became more aware of women gazing out passenger-seat windows with looks of complete despair, and I would find myself wanting to do something about it.

One of my employees was repeatedly abused, not only by her husband but by her teenage son as well, which was hard to comprehend. She finally agreed to let me put her up in a local hotel until we could find a shelter. I thought she would enjoy sitting in bed with freedom and a television remote for a few nights to catch her breath, but in no time, she returned back home out of fear. It made no sense to me—to be drawn toward fear rather than away from it.

There was another incident when the elderly mother of one of my employees was facing eviction from government housing right before Christmas, which seemed so tragic. She was disabled from years of severe abuse and unable to work. I secretly paid her rent and was shocked that it cost only fifty dollars to keep this woman off the streets during Christmas, when some people spent the same amount getting their nails done.

Truly, there was a world I did not realize was out there. But that wasn't the only world to which I would be introduced.

———

Okay, so this is a part of the story I have shared with only a few before now. And quite frankly, it makes me uncomfortable to share it here. For many years, every time I told the story of how Blue Monarch got started, I walked away feeling like I'd left out a big, secret part. My fear was that people would say, "You have lost all credibility with me," even though I knew others would say, "I hate it when that happens." Regardless, I feel a nudge to share this special part of the story now. So here goes . . . I suppose after this we might as well go through my underwear drawer.

It was about 4:00 in the morning on April Fool's Day when I got a phone call. Naturally I thought there must be a family emergency, but it was my baker, Linda, calling me from The Blue Chair. She had shown up to begin baking and was shocked at what she found when she unlocked the door.

The big, massive ovens were on full blast, the kitchen was so blistering hot that plastic was beginning to melt, and pots and pans were scattered all over the floor as if they had been thrown in a fit of anger. None of this made any sense. Linda had turned off the alarm when she'd opened the door, and the alarm company later confirmed I had been the last one to set it the night before, when I locked up. No one had entered until Linda got to work that morning.

There was no reasonable explanation for what had happened, and it left us a little shell-shocked the rest of the day. Little did I know, this was just a preview of what would happen later that night, which began with a dream.

I dreamt I was at The Blue Chair talking with Linda about what had happened earlier that morning. Suddenly, in the dream, for no apparent reason, I became so overwhelmed with fear that I dropped to the floor. That's when I woke up.

Clay had retreated to the living room earlier because he had been snoring. All of a sudden, the bedroom filled with an unexplainable thick darkness. I could no longer see the light at the barn, which was alarming. Was I suddenly blind? A tremendous weight held me down, making it impossible to move, difficult to breathe, and impossible to speak. I felt a dark presence over me, and somehow, with no spoken words, "it" and I immediately began communicating back and forth.

"I am not afraid of you!" was the message I sent. This was a lie, because I was more frightened than I had ever been in my entire life.

"Oh, you don't think you are afraid? You just wait..."

At that point, this "thing" began breathing on the top of my head. I could hear a deep, very slow and deliberate, raspy gust of air that was hot on my scalp. It breathed in and out, in and out. Long, hot, deep breaths. For a second, I wondered if this was how I was going to die, and if anyone would ever know why. I feared this thing was trying to suck my soul right out of my body.

I began praying, "God, please deliver me from this thing! Please help me!"

At that moment, I could tell that I was about to see something materialize in front of my eyes, illuminated in the total darkness. It was something that looked indistinguishable and blurry, as if under water, and I was afraid that when it became clearer it would be the face of this hideous thing still breathing on my head. *Please no, I don't want to see its face!*

Shockingly, when the vision materialized, it was a massive, glorious angel filled with and surrounded by bright white light. I remember thinking in that moment, *Wow, angels are real!* The angel was magnificent and had its massive wings stretched out on either side. It was beautiful and breathtaking. *What is happening?!* For a second, I wondered if I had died.

Next, the angel faded away, and once again I could tell something was about to materialize in front of my eyes. I was still afraid I would see the face of this evil thing lurking over me. When the vision became clearer, it was the angel again, except this time it was turned to the side with its head and fists tucked to its chest as if in a powerful, fighting, charge position.

The angel quickly disappeared, and at the exact same moment, the darkness whisked out of the room, making an unfamiliar sound as it left. My body instantly felt so much lighter, I honestly thought I might float above the bed. *Lord, please no, I don't think I can take that too.* I looked out the window and saw the light on at the barn once again. My dog, Cooper, was snoring on the floor as if nothing had ever happened. It felt so good to take a deep breath.

For many weeks I processed what I had experienced and was afraid to share it with anyone, lest they think I was losing my mind. I collected crosses everywhere I went and hung one in every empty spot I could find. For quite a while, even though I knew God had protected me, I cautiously went to bed each night wondering if I might encounter such a visitor again. I prayed like never before, and passages in the Bible suddenly came to life in a brand-new way. *"For our struggle is not against flesh and blood, but against the rulers, against the authorities, against the powers of this dark world and against the spiritual forces of evil in the heavenly realms"* (Ephesians 6:12). I felt I had been intimately introduced to a level of darkness I had never known, or even believed, existed.

The thing that made no sense was, what in the world had I done to attract that kind of attention? I was just minding my own business, living in the middle of the woods, running a tiny little bakery.

Six weeks later I had my answer.

———

We had just survived the University of the South graduation weekend in Sewanee, which was the biggest weekend of the year, and we closed the bakery for a few days since most of the town had vanished with school out. I was relaxing in a hammock on the bluff where we live, just basking in the glow of our success and imagining ways to solve our biggest problem, which was that we were absolutely bursting at the seams. *How can we expand our business when we have such a tiny space?*

Maybe we should have a commercial kitchen at another location to produce more product. Hey, I know. Maybe we can offer jobs to the women who have struggled so much. But that won't solve their problems. They probably need some services to overcome their issues at home. And wouldn't it be great if they could also live there? . . . And what if it was also a safe place for them to live with their children? . . . I was on a roll.

Wait a minute. Holy cow . . . that is exactly what was described in that powerful dream years ago. Time stood still as this overwhelming thought gradually sank in.

This is totally unexplainable, but in that very moment, a large amount of water splashed onto my face. No kidding. In fact, my first thought was that it must have come from some enormous bird, so I looked up, but saw no bird.

As I wiped the water off my face, I began to understand what was happening. *Oh my word. This must be why I found myself here. And this must be what God is asking me to do. He must have thought it would take a bucket of water to get my attention.*

It was overwhelming and made no sense. *Why me?* No doubt, God must have asked a lot of people who turned him down before getting around to me, and that was not a good sign. After all, I had successfully avoided eye contact with him since I was a child—specifically so he would never ask me to do something like this. I had not really attended church in seven years. Had he not noticed? And was he not aware I had been married three times? Surely, he wasn't happy about that. God had obviously made a terrible mistake.

For three days I cried because it felt so huge, and I felt incredibly unworthy and unqualified. In fact, I often call this my three days in the belly of the fish. I was also exhausted from running my business, and I couldn't imagine such a huge undertaking on top of that.

But it was something my seventeen-year-old daughter said that made all the difference. Even as a small child, she had been way more spiritually mature than I was. After seeing me struggle and agonize over this decision, she finally said, "You know, Mommy, you can tell God no. God won't love you any less than if you say yes."

That had never occurred to me, and it literally stopped me in my tracks.

I don't think I had even realized I had a choice. How could I say no to a God like that?

Here is another part of the story I don't always share. Perhaps it feels too personal. But when I realized what God was asking me to do, I also felt in my heart that he was asking me to do something that would ultimately take my life. Literally. I didn't know how it would happen, but I believed in my spirit the assignment would kill me at some point. But do you know what is interesting? Once I said yes, I never had that feeling again. I don't know if it was a test, or if it no longer mattered to me, but that thought never returned.

Naturally, if I was going to take this on, I wanted to do it on my own terms. I told God, "Yes, I will do this, but on one condition. I will never, ever speak in public." Two weeks later I was in front of a Rotary Club and thought I might throw up.

There was a day when I sat at our computer and in one sitting, over three hours, I wrote the entire business plan for the new organization. It was a supernatural experience because when I looked back at what I had written, it included detailed information regarding issues I knew nothing about. Through God's supernatural intervention, it had turned into the book from my dream, but was not as thick, so I figured the rest would come later.

The organization needed a name, of course, so one day I spent considerable time researching the characteristics of different butterflies. It seemed, for obvious reasons, that a butterfly accurately represented the transformation process women would experience, and I wanted to find the best fit. Later that evening as I sat on the sofa doing payroll for my business, there was a movie playing on the television in the background that caught my attention. I heard a man say, "You see this butterfly? You know what's special about it?"

You are kidding me. Is everyone's TV saying this right now?

He pointed to a beautiful butterfly on a tree branch and said, "This is a monarch. They are special because they survive the winter when others don't. They are fragile, yet so determined." Perfect. Blue was my favorite color and was also included in the name of my business, so naturally I had to throw that in too. That's when the name Blue Monarch was born.

Since the Grundy County High School building had been in my dream, I assumed this was where Blue Monarch should be located. I imagined turning classrooms into apartments and designed the whole facility in my head and on paper. I even took Lisa, the amazing mural artist who helped me at The Blue Chair, through the building to see how we might make the hallways look like neighborhood streets and the classrooms look like small cottages.

For four months I attended every city council meeting to present my plan, which I expected to be eagerly embraced. But I walked away disappointed each time. More than once, someone said, "Why would we want to put those women and children in there when something better might come along?" This hurt my heart because I could not imagine any better occupant than women and children who were suffering. There were a couple of open-minded individuals who privately supported my idea, but ultimately I gave up on the building and walked away feeling very discouraged and defeated. In fact, I convinced myself that God had not really asked me to do this thing after all and that I must think an awful lot of myself to have imagined it. The pieces were not falling into place, and it was time to let go of this outlandish idea.

Just inches away from abandoning the project, I stepped across the street from my bakery one day to get the mail. Right away, I noticed a card that had come all the way from California. Interesting. The card said, "You don't know me, but my daughter is a student at Sewanee, and she told me what you're trying to do. Please use this money in any way you can to get started." Shockingly, a sweet woman named Libby had put $1,000 cash in that card, and it had survived all the way across the country. My eyes immediately teared up, and I had to accept the fact that perhaps this thing had a life of its own and I must not lose faith. I have told Libby several times since then that her gift was probably the most important donation we ever received, because I had been so close to giving up.

Since I could not have the building I wanted, I decided to have an open mind and draw the perfect plan on paper. It was a place out in the country, with three homes on it, and I had a plan for each house. Then I went on a big search to find it.

I looked at another empty school building, a creepy abandoned hospital that still had blood on the floor, and a handful of other unsuitable properties. Finally, I heard of a bed-and-breakfast for sale. The price had just been reduced.

When I drove in, I could not believe what I found. It was fifty acres in the country, with three houses on it, and even better, it came completely furnished because the owners were moving to Israel. It was ten times better than anything I could have imagined—it had a pool, a barn, a herd of sheep, and asparagus ready to be harvested. It had all the dishes, pots and pans, linens, lawn mower, basically everything we needed to get started. It was breathtaking.

I needed to be honest with the owners and let them know I was not a qualified buyer and had a lot to figure out before I could purchase the property. So I shared my entire story with Pam and Denny. After I finished, I expected them to chastise me for wasting their time cutting all that grass. But, surprisingly, with tears in her eyes, Pam said, "We always knew God had asked us to build this place for someone else to use one day—and we always thought it would be for women who were hurting. We're just glad you finally showed up." Still gives me chills after all these years.

It was the perfect place, but how could we possibly pay for it? It was nearly a million dollars. Well, that is where the Grundy County High School building actually played a critical role.

On one of those many walks through the empty high school building, I met a nice man named Russ. After I shared my idea with him, he invited me to a Rotary meeting to tell the same story to the group. He also wanted me to meet his good friend Howell, a gentleman from Atlanta who had helped start the Grundy County Rotary. Russ thought Howell would be interested in my idea because he and his family had owned property in nearby Beersheba for many years, and he had a strong passion for the people in the area.

Despite obvious stranger danger, I got in a car with this man I had just met and rode with him to Coalmont to present my plan to his Rotary Club. About halfway there, I realized my cell phone was still in my car but would probably be useless anyway in such a remote area. No one knew I was with this man. I made sure my door was unlocked, just in case I needed to make a quick getaway.

Eventually we pulled into the parking lot at the Rotary meeting, and Howell was there. I was relieved about both. Howell loved my plan to help women and children and gave me a lot of encouragement. He asked me to send him more information, which I did.

Later, when Howell learned about the bed-and-breakfast property, he made a trip to see it, and after he talked it over with his wife, Madeline, they offered to help me buy it. Even though I was basically a stranger with nothing more than an ambitious plan on paper, Madeline and Howell offered to borrow the near million dollars at a very low interest rate, and we would be responsible for the note payments. It was a risk for them and a miracle for us. (Thankfully, we paid this off ten years later.)

We had the perfect place and a way to purchase the property, but how would we make the monthly payments?

An advisory board was quickly assembled, and a tour of the property was arranged. Perhaps they could help me raise the money we needed to commit to the note payments. I was excited to show off the ideal, picturesque setting for Blue Monarch, but the overall lack of enthusiasm was not what I expected. Two of the advisory board members pulled me aside and said, "Don't you think this place is a little too nice for them?"

This caused a knee-jerk reaction, and I said, "Is it too nice for your own daughters? Oh, and by the way, you are no longer on the advisory board." That the place was so nice was part of what made it so perfect. I wanted the women and children to know that others believed they deserved a nice place to live. And to this day, many of the women burst into tears when they see our campus for the first time. Their kids are proud to call it home.

It turns out, there was an unexpected solution to my dilemma. During the two years I stood behind the counter each day at my bakery, there was a young man who came in every morning for his usual cappuccino. He was not a student but always sat there sipping on his coffee drink while reading a book. His hair was often a little messy, but he typically wore very nice shoes. He was quiet, very kind, extremely polite, and quite mysterious. In fact, we wrote "Mysterious Ben" on his ticket when he placed an order.

One morning Mysterious Ben was in the shop, and I heard this overwhelming message over and over in my head. "Go share your plan with Ben. Go share your plan with Ben." I had my business plan with me, so I finally went over to him and said, "Ben, I can't explain why, but I feel I need to share this idea with you. Here is a description, and you can take a look if you'd like. I'd love to get your thoughts."

He graciously took the binder from me and in one sitting carefully read it from cover to cover. He then asked if he could take it home with him. Seemed strange, but okay.

For two weeks Ben came in every morning with a specific question about how we might solve certain problems, what would we do about this or that? Finally, he asked if he could see the property we wanted to purchase.

Felt a little odd, but I made an appointment, and we walked the property for quite some time. Finally, I said, "Ben, I give up. What do you have in mind?"

"Well, my family has a foundation, and the women in my family run it, but they sometimes look to me for ideas of where to put their money. I think they would be very blessed to be a part of this on the front end." They ended up giving us a sizable gift each year for the first three years, which was more than enough to make the note payments.

We closed on the property in March of 2003 and took possession a month later, on April 15, not even a year after my revelation on the bluff when the water hit my face. Since that time, we have served almost a thousand women and children. There are also hundreds of children who have been reunited with their mothers who had previously lost custody. I have seen miracles that take my breath away and healing that can only be explained as supernatural. To this day, Blue Monarch has never strayed from the original plan described in my dream—right down to the women having employment by producing a product. That product is Out of the Blue Granola, which is sold in major grocery chains and specialty stores across our region.

So there you have it. A long answer to a short question. What made me want to do something like this? I have discovered it is impossible to make anyone want something. We cannot make someone want recovery. Neither can we make a mother want a better relationship with her children. We have to allow her to figure out on her own that she wants it. And that is exactly what God did for me.

He placed a burden on my heart for the women and children we serve, he blindfolded me and led me to the perfect property, he introduced key people to make it happen, and then he escorted me to a front row seat at the greatest show on earth. Who in her right mind would not want that?

Some of the amazing women and children of Blue Monarch
Photo credit: Michelle Barnett Photography

"THAT'S ONE HELLUVA PRAYER."

My journey with Blue Monarch has been filled with wonderful memories as well as some painful bumps along the way. When God asked me to take this on, I had absolutely no idea what I was getting myself into. And when I think back, my expectations were so incredibly low. I just had *no* idea.

This could not have been clearer to me than when I witnessed the birth of our first Blue Monarch baby. It was our first year, and our program was brand-new. As an artist with no social-work background, I was just figuring things out as we went along. One of our first residents showed up pregnant. She hid it well, because we didn't know she was expecting a baby until her water broke, which came as quite a surprise.

Chrystal was way too early to be going into labor, so she was rushed to the hospital for thirty days of bed rest. During this time, I frequently traveled to Chattanooga to visit her, bringing lots of reading material and trying to structure some kind of productive program for her under the circumstances.

One thing I noticed was that this young woman was beginning to develop a personal relationship with God—which seemed pretty remarkable considering she was alone in her room most of the time, confined to the bed with very little to keep her busy.

Way before the thirty days were up, Chrystal called me one day and said, "Miss Susan, you've got to get here right away. I have to have an emergency C-section!"

As soon as I arrived, I was suited up for the C-section, completely shocked they allowed ordinary people off the street to witness this dramatic surgery. But when the doctor lifted the baby out, I was horrified because he looked like a little dead bird. He was black from the knees down and looked completely lifeless. Fortunately, the mother was not able to see what I saw. They immediately whisked him away, and we returned to Chrystal's room to wait for news. We waited... and waited... and waited. Three painful hours went by, and not one person could tell us anything about the baby. I noticed the nurses were avoiding eye contact. Things didn't look good.

Finally, the young doctor entered the room and said, "We've tried everything to save your baby, but we're not going to be able to. So if you want to see him alive, you only have a few minutes left." I was taken aback by the doctor's bedside manner in such a traumatic moment, and immediately assumed he must be conditioned from seeing this scene so often.

As you can imagine, our world turned upside down in a split second. Chrystal was extremely upset, and the entire NICU cleared out so we could visit her baby in privacy during his last moments. This time he looked like a dead bird in a box hooked up to a million wires. He was pitiful and tiny and lifeless.

The doctor pointed to a gauge overhead and said, "You see this number? This measures his blood oxygen level and should be over 90. But as you can see, it's only 20."

After an understandable emotional breakdown, Chrystal decided to go back to her room because she did not want to watch her baby die. But it definitely did not feel right to leave him alone, so I stayed with him. I stuck my finger into an opening in his box and was surprised that even in his fragile state, he wrapped his tiny little hand around my finger. With Christmas only a few days away, Christmas carols were quietly playing in the background, which only made this moment even more surreal.

What in the world was happening? I thought I was going to help women get jobs, and I was about to watch a little baby die. I was angry with God in that moment and felt he had not been up front with me about the assignment I had been given. "This was not in the brochure!"

I watched the dreaded number continue to drop from 20... to 16... and then all the way down to 11.

Suddenly it occurred to me that we needed to be praying for this baby! So I got on the phone, called my daughter in the middle of the night, and asked her to call all her friends and start praying for a miracle.

Even though I had grown up in the church, I had heard about "the power of prayer" until it no longer meant anything. I couldn't imagine how it could possibly make a difference at this point, but I sat next to the baby and prayed anyway as I listened to the Christmas music and braced myself for his inevitable death. I prayed hard, but I will admit, my faith was not even the size of a mustard seed.

Afraid of what I might see, I eventually peeked at the gauge, and much to my surprise, the number had begun to rise. It was back up to 20. *Wow. Maybe it moves around?* I kept watching as that number gradually climbed all the way up to over 90 again! It was unbelievable!

The nurses ran over to me and could not believe what they saw. They quickly fetched the doctor, and when he rushed over, he looked at me and demanded, "What did you do?!"

"I really don't know. We just have a lot of folks praying for this baby."

"Well, that's one helluva prayer team you people have! I've never seen anything like this!"

Chrystal named the baby Trenton, but the nurses called him "the Christmas Miracle Baby" the rest of the time he was there.

Little did I know, that would not be our last miracle—not by a long shot—because we were in the business of saving lives.

"WHY IS *HEAL* A FOUR-LETTER WORD?"

Have you ever noticed how addiction tends to be a sensitive topic? It seems everyone has strong opinions about how to fix the problem, and many experts believe they hold the key to the mint. But the debate over a cure seems to have many still scratching their heads.

I do not claim to be an expert on addiction. In fact, after many years of dealing with addiction up close and personal on a daily basis, I am still quite puzzled by it.

I have often tried to get into the head of an addict and imagine how it must feel to have absolutely no willpower to resist a temptation of some sort, even when it has devastating consequences. Honestly, with the exception of eating an entire pan of Christmas fudge until my eyes swelled shut or justifying every single biscuit until I had eaten an entire batch in one sitting, I really cannot relate to what addiction feels like. I was not willing to choose fudge or biscuits over my child, and I never went out purposefully looking for them either.

I am no expert on the subject. But I am an expert on what I have personally observed over many years as we have dealt with struggling, addicted women. Through this powerful experience, I have established some pretty strong opinions of my own. I realize some folks will adamantly disagree with me, and others will wholeheartedly agree, but hey—this is what I have seen with my own two eyes.

There are so many theories floating around about addiction:

- "It is a disease that can never be cured."
- "Once you're an addict, you're always an addict."

- "Some people are just genetically wired to be addicts and can't help it."

Sometimes people battling addiction are told these things for so long, they label themselves as addicts for life. This not only crushes all hope for a cure, but it sometimes gives them an excuse for their behavior. "Well, I can't help it. I'm an addict, and that's what addicts do."

We believe there is a difference between *sobriety* and *freedom*. We can easily provide sobriety. It's the freedom we're interested in.

We see women who began using drugs for a laundry list of reasons. Here are just a few:

- "My mother and grandmother taught me to use drugs."
- "I had surgery, and the doctor prescribed me painkillers. Then I couldn't live without them."
- "I tried drugs one time out of curiosity, and I've been chasing that first high ever since."

This list could go on and on. But see what it tells you? There is not a cookie-cutter addict out there. They begin using drugs for all kinds of reasons. So how can you treat each one the same?

That is why I am so grateful for our program and the flexibility it provides as a privately funded nonprofit. When we see that something works, we can implement it that same day. We can have a good idea at a 10:00 a.m. staff meeting and be doing it by that afternoon. We are constantly improving what we do to meet the individual needs of each and every woman we serve.

Therefore, we address addiction in a variety of ways because we are treating a cluster of issues. We look at the core reasons why each woman started using drugs in the first place. This is discovered through counseling and the recovery curriculum we use that focuses on thinking errors and criminal behavior. We look at the wounds that possibly led to drugs and then work on forgiveness and self-esteem. We study relationships and how to avoid unhealthy ones in the future. When family members are not good for one's recovery, we work on how to establish healthy boundaries.

But this is what we believe truly brings freedom: We believe one can be healed from addiction. Yes, I said it. Healed.

I have always thought it made absolutely no sense that God would scratch his head and say, "I can heal all kinds of diseases, but that addiction thing really has me stumped." In fact, in Matthew 9:35, the Bible tells of how Jesus went all over "healing every disease and sickness." Can you imagine if Jesus had said, "All you addicts, I'm sorry. I cannot help you. The rest of you, over here."

Psalm 103:2–5 says: *"Praise the Lord, my soul, and forget not all his benefits—who forgives all your sins and heals all your diseases, who redeems your life from the pit and crowns you with love and compassion, who satisfies your desires with good things so that your youth is renewed like the eagle's."*

Just to be sure, I asked some experts recently if they felt they had truly been healed of their drug addictions. They just happened to be several incredible women on our amazing staff.

Each one described how she had been healed through her personal relationship with Jesus Christ—and each one described how she no longer had any cravings whatsoever for drugs. One had even been unexpectedly exposed to her drug of choice, and just the idea of it sickened her. Would that not be the definition of healing—when the desire is completely gone? Not just managed—but gone! These pictures show what true freedom looks like, and

we want that for every woman we serve, because with freedom comes joy.

So is addiction a disease? Do some people have a defective gene that makes them addicts no matter what? Truth is, it really doesn't matter. We can stop people from using drugs in lots and lots of ways.

Staff members Kate Cataldo, Dona Masters, and Jeannie Driver Campbell

22

That has been proven. But the true cure has been right before our very eyes this whole time ...

"for I, the Lord, am your healer." (Exodus 15:26 NASB)

Thank you, Lord, for a place where women discover that it's possible to heal, not only from emotional wounds and traumas, but even from addiction. Thank you for the true freedom that is only found in you. Amen.

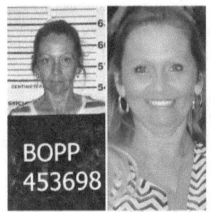

Dona Masters' dramatic before and after

"WHAT A HOLY MESS."

One of my earliest and most difficult lessons through Blue Monarch took place the first time a resident left early. It was 2004, and at that time our curriculum was twelve months long. (It is now a one-to-three-year program and individually structured.)

Jeannie was our poster child. She came to us directly from jail in our very first year. She had three daughters and was able to be reunited with them through our program. Jeannie was not only beautiful inside and out—she was also smart and capable of doing great things. She developed a strong relationship with God, improved her parenting skills, and even got a job in a nursing home helping the elderly, which she loved. As far as I could tell, she was a perfect example of what Blue Monarch was supposed to provide and how women could expect to transform their lives while they were with us. Yep, that was a job well done for all of us.

Jeannie Driver Campbell with her daughters, Carmen, Samara, and Jayda

So when Jeannie decided to leave after only six months, I was devastated. I thought it was a terrible mistake because I knew she wasn't ready, but she was so hardheaded she would not listen. That made me angry. I remember standing in Jeannie's upstairs room trying to reason with her while she packed, and it ended in a heated argument because we were both so emotional. Jeannie felt she had accomplished all she had come to Blue Monarch to do, and she was ready to go back to her old friends and change them as well. She was invincible—or at least that's what she thought.

24

Being new to addiction and recovery, even I knew that was a terrible mistake. I couldn't imagine it working the way she thought it would. But she left anyway. Feeling utterly defeated and heartbroken, I began to wonder if Blue Monarch was a complete failure. It looked like a holy mess to me.

It wasn't long after that when I ran into Jeannie's prosecutor, Steve. I shared with him my disappointing news about Jeannie, and he patiently listened to me. When I finished, he said, "You tell that story as if it's a failure. To me, it's still a success story."

"How can you say that? She was only with us for six months, and she left when she wasn't ready. We failed her."

"Well, the way I see it," he said, "for six months she was not on the streets selling drugs. And for six months her children were exposed to a much better way of life. That to me is a success."

This revelation completely changed the way I looked at our program after that. I began to consider what could have taken place during those six months if Jeannie and her girls had not been with us. The possibilities were endless, and the potential for disaster was great. I eventually came to understand that even if someone leaves our program early, they still gain something valuable while they are with us. And I now have a box full of letters women have sent me to confirm just that.

Some of those letters are from Jeannie. Her plan to change her friends failed miserably and quickly. She ended up in federal prison for four years, and during that time we stayed in touch. I even remember meeting her at Waffle House in the middle of the night when she was transported from one prison to another to participate in an intensive recovery program there. It was great to see her, but it hurt to think of her being separated from her girls for so long and wasting all that time in prison. Again, it looked like a holy mess to me.

During those four years, though, Jeannie developed and strengthened her faith and worked diligently to become the woman Christ intended her to be. It was a beautiful thing to witness as she described her journey through the letters she wrote.

All those years in prison, Jeannie expressed to me that she would love to find a way to help Blue Monarch one day. She always felt Blue Monarch was a special place and that she and her children had developed a lasting bond here. She often said their time with us had probably prevented a devastating crisis for all of them. (Guess her prosecutor was right.)

After she was released and was settled back into the real world, Jeannie began coming to our campus every Friday night to conduct a Bible study with our residents. Right away it became evident that Jeannie was able to offer something the rest of us could not. And it was something very valuable.

One of my greatest dreams has now come true. Because of a surprising and amazing gift from some generous folks, we have been able to hire Jeannie and add her to our amazing team at Blue Monarch. More than once I have heard Jeannie described as someone who "just lights up the room." Yes, I would agree. She glows with the light of the Holy Spirit. We are blessed that God took Jeannie's personal journey that was painful and difficult, and found a way to bless others in a way that only he can do.

Now, when I hear Jeannie talking to our residents with such great compassion and rich understanding that only she can offer, I am reminded in living color how God can take what appears to be a holy mess and turn it into a holy blessing. I just have to wonder . . . what looks like a holy mess to me today?

"THIS ISN'T MY STAIN!"

It was as if God said, "You know what? I think you need to walk in her shoes for a while. In fact, maybe for the next three nights."

God often speaks to me in my dreams, but this was one I could have done without. At the beginning of this dream, I was in jail being booked for some crime—but for what? It was a vivid, very realistic dream in which I had just undergone a humiliating body search, which left me feeling extremely embarrassed and violated. The ink on my fingertips made me feel marked and branded. I remember looking at my fingerprints and saying to myself, "Well, this is the only thing that proves I'm an individual, because now I am just a number."

Standing for a mug shot, I held my number in front of me while fighting back tears, and immediately pictured my photo in the local paper where everyone I knew would see it. I thought I might throw up. It even occurred to me that the numbers behind my head would tell the whole world how tall I was. Not sure why that even mattered—it just felt like one more violation.

The. Shame. Was. Unbearable.

Even though I did not seem to have any kind of awareness of the crime I had committed, I cannot describe the deep, intense humiliation and shame I felt. Nothing I had ever experienced even came close to it. But this one moment somehow seemed to wipe out anything positive I had ever done in my life. I saw how the officers looked at me with total indifference, and then I realized I had become completely insignificant. They were joking among themselves about something totally unrelated to my crisis, and it hit me, this was just another day at the office for them while it felt like the end of the world for me.

I woke up in a cold sweat, relieved to discover I was still at home in my own bed. I spent the entire day sort of rattled and afraid that maybe my dream was a warning I was about to get into some kind of trouble. It was so real! So I began paying much more attention to the speed limit and vowed to drive more safely, since that was the only thing I could think of that might get me into trouble. Even speeding wouldn't get me arrested unless I hurt someone, so was that about to happen?

Unfortunately, the next night another dream picked up where the last one left off. I was back in the same jail and could smell the stale odor of too many bodies in an enclosed space with still air. It's an unpleasant smell that seems to live at every jail I have ever visited while interviewing potential residents for Blue Monarch. I have always wondered, do jail workers bring it home on their clothes?

They handed me the orange jumpsuit and "whites" that I had to wear, and I could only imagine who and how many had worn them before me. Having a personal sense of style had always been important to me, so handing my carefully chosen jewelry and clothing to someone to store in a paper bag seemed like the last handoff for who I was as an individual. Little by little, drip by drip, I was truly becoming a nobody. A worthless nobody.

I was then taken to my cell, which I would share with a stranger, and right off the bat I realized there was no such thing as privacy anymore. The nasty toilet was out in the open for the whole world to see. At that point I actually wanted to be nobody and simply disappear. I felt overwhelmingly empty and hopeless, and even crying didn't seem to make it better. I looked around and realized there was no place to go for comfort. It felt just as bad in every corner of the cell.

Then I woke up. Thank goodness.

That I had this sort of dream two nights in a row was really unsettling. Surely I was about to get arrested for something. I continued to watch the speed limit, because that was all I knew to do.

Well, you guessed it. The third night picked up right where the last dream left off. Except this time the humiliation and shame escalated to a whole new level.

A group of us were lined up to go to court. Our hands and feet were shackled together, so even walking was embarrassing because it was impossible to do so with any kind of dignity, taking baby steps and lined up like cattle.

When we walked into court, I was devastated and wanted to crawl into a hole. I was especially embarrassed to be in public without any makeup, and my highlights were beginning to grow out, leaving terrible dark roots. (I know, I feel pretty shallow admitting it.)

My orange jumpsuit was permanently soiled—and from what, I didn't care to know. I wanted to announce, "This isn't my stain!" The long-sleeved white T-shirt underneath was more of a dingy gray color, and my scratchy socks had holes in them that were visible in the oversized plastic shoes I was required to wear. I was cold. The temperature, along with my anxiety, made me shake uncontrollably.

We paraded into the courtroom in single file, and as I looked out across the room, I immediately recognized people I knew—some were people I just happened to know from the community who looked shocked to see me. Others were friends and family members who had expressions on their faces that were a complicated combination of disgust, anger, disappointment, hurt, grief, and even their own personal humiliation, which I knew I had caused.

There really aren't any words strong enough for what I felt. The deep regret, the excruciating heartache, the agonizing shame, the anger toward myself, and the extreme hopelessness were so intense I thought I might pass out. I cried and then struggled to wipe my eyes, which was hard to do with my hands connected to my feet, so I finally decided to let the tears just run down my face. What difference did it make anyway?

Thankfully, I woke up in a sweat. Sitting on the edge of my bed, I struggled to understand why I had been taken on this terrible journey over the past three nights. What could it mean? *Please, Lord, what are you trying to tell me? And please make it stop.*

Truth is, as time passed and I was greatly relieved to see that my jail dreams did not come true, I realized they had taught me a lot. I have reflected back on them many times since then. Some of the lessons were obvious:

- God needed me to really *feel* how impossible it seems when the journey out of hopelessness and despair looks so steep. That road to recovery is extremely long and difficult, so I must respect the process and never take it lightly.
- He needed me to *feel* the level of shame our women experience so I would know how important it is for them to receive constant encouragement and praise over even the smallest accomplishments. Words matter—and they matter as individuals.
- I needed to *feel* how tempting it was to become hardened and indifferent in order to avoid appearing weak and vulnerable. So we must be patient, as it will take time to trust us.

But this is the lesson I did not get until today:

In my dreams I never knew what crime I had committed, which has always been a little puzzling to me. After all, wouldn't that affect the circumstances and outcome? So today as I prayed for further understanding of these powerful and graphic dreams, I revisited this question. Suddenly God pointed something out to me, which I now see is the most valuable lesson of all:

He is not concerned about the crime. He cares about the heart.

What is important to God is that we understand we are new creations through Christ and that the old self is gone. And that is what we must never forget to teach the amazing women we serve. Only then does the shame truly go away. After all, in God's eyes no one is a nobody. No one. Not ever.

> *Therefore, if anyone is in Christ, the new creation has come: The old has gone, the new is here! All this is from God, who reconciled us to himself through Christ and gave us the ministry of reconciliation: that God was reconciling the world to himself in Christ, not counting people's sins against them.* (2 Corinthians 5:17–19)

"I'M HOLDING THE KEY, AND I'M NOT AFRAID TO USE IT."

It was in the beginning years when I wore nearly every hat and I was desperate for help. There were several nights when I jumped out of bed at 2:00 in the morning and rushed down to Blue Monarch because someone had activated a panic button. Or even worse, the silent holdup alarm, which would get pushed over and over—you guessed it, because it was silent. The alarm company had no details, so my mind would imagine all kinds of disasters on my forty-five-minute drive, which felt like an eternity. Nearly every time, there was no true emergency, but for lack of a better system, and lack of adequate staff, I had no choice but to check it out myself just in case. After a rash of these incidents and lots of lost sleep, a missionary couple approached me about a live-in position, and from their résumés, they looked ideal—an answered prayer.

Right when they walked in for the interview, I noticed the man's silver belt buckle, which formed an ornate butterfly. My immediate, knee-jerk reaction was to say under my breath, "Well, that's rather clever, Satan." I knew in my heart this was just a trick to mislead me, so what did I do? I hired them. It was crazy. Everyone else saw the belt buckle as "a sign" from God, and because I was so desperate for help, I ignored my gut, listened to others, and hired the couple anyway.

Well, you can guess the outcome. It was a disaster. The man with the butterfly belt buckle ended up in jail for fraud committed elsewhere about a year after I fired him.

When I look back at the lowest points in my Blue Monarch journey, I cannot deny the obvious. There is a definite theme that ties those experiences together. Every single time we suffered as an organization, or I suffered as a leader, it was because I let down my guard and failed as the gatekeeper. Being in a state of desperation and exhaustion only causes us to ignore the "Warning, warning!" in our ear, and it is the absolute worst time to make a major decision.

When other, similar ministries visit with us to pick our brains, I always warn the leader, "Your most important job is to be the gatekeeper." I then proceed to give examples of all the times I allowed the wrong people to come through the door, which caused negativity, division, and even chaos. Oddly enough, these things never came from the population we served. It was always those who had been given positions of authority. And many times, it was because I settled for less, believing I could not find better. In other words, I did not have the patience to wait on God for the right people.

I have discovered that the role of gatekeeper extends way beyond just finding the best board members or hiring the most appropriate individuals. It has also become very clear to me that we are just as responsible for guarding the minds and hearts of the vulnerable women and children we serve. We have a duty to protect them. They trust us with their lives.

Let me tell you about one example. And I will give you a heads-up: it ventures into an area that is a little supernatural and may include information you will wish you could unhear.

Our policies are constantly evolving, and the list gets longer and longer—every single rule is the result of a bad experience. For instance, there was a day when I pulled up at Blue Monarch and found all the women and children on the roof. Turns out, "It was such a great place to think." Who knew? Well, there's a new rule. #32: No climbing out on the roof.

But one day many years ago, I discovered we needed another rule regarding books and movies. Apparently, this was an area we had overlooked, and as a result, there were hundreds of inappropriate books and very scary, disturbing, X-rated, and even unrated movies that had somehow found their way into our houses. I realize at this point I am running the risk of sounding like a prude, but none of what we found was something our children needed to be exposed to, and they didn't offer anything positive for the women either. In fact, our residents admitted the books and movies immediately took them back to another place and time—the very ones they had come to Blue Monarch to escape.

I was especially disturbed to learn that a specific woman (we will call her Kellie) had been allowed to collect numerous books about real-life serial killers. Apparently, a staff member, who no longer works with us, had allowed her to do so because she thought it was therapeutic to encourage something this woman found "stimulating." Well, I thought this was outrageous.

Kellie suffered from severe PTSD. As a young child she witnessed the sacrifice of another child, her same age, during a satanic ritual. Can you imagine? (I will spare you any more details.) The trauma from that was overwhelming and was forever burned into her memory, and it would take nothing less than God's tremendous power of healing to overcome such a horrific experience. How were we helping her by filling her mind with dark, detailed, disturbing stories about murderers? What in the world? (The family member who exposed her to this atrocity had already died, so I was denied the pleasure of pursuing criminal charges.)

The women and children we serve show up with minds that are filled with ugly memories and ideas, almost as if their thoughts are muddy. But we want their thoughts and feelings to become crystal clear, filled with as much joy and hope as we can possibly muster up. Remarkably, this is a gradual process that we can tangibly see on their faces when they replace the mud with good and positive thoughts instead. The women actually become more beautiful. Ask anyone working at Blue Monarch, and they will agree. But there's more. Even their children begin to come alive in a way that is truly incredible.

*Blue Monarch child
with Sam, our dog*

That's what I wanted for Kellie, but we let her down by allowing even more darkness and fear to fill her head with grotesque stories to dwell on and dream about. Didn't she have enough of that already? So, after apologizing to this young woman, we did a complete overhaul of all the books and movies on the property. Sadly, our confiscated bounty filled an enormous box. I put the box in the trunk of my car and planned to burn it all when I got home.

My husband made a good point though. It would make a sticky mess with all the plastic, so I agreed to find a convenience center on my way to a meeting in Nashville the following day.

Well, I attempted four different convenience centers along my route, and all were closed. I still had the disgusting books and movies in my car when I stopped at a congested, very large intersection in Nashville. This is where it gets a little weird.

As I was sitting still at the red light, I suddenly noticed up in the sky an enormous, larger-than-life-size, solid-black bird making a nosedive straight toward my windshield like a speeding torpedo. It looked about the size of a large pelican. Out of instinct I ducked, just in time to see the strange creature violently bust a hole in my windshield with its beak and bounce off out of sight. I tried to see where it landed, but couldn't find it.

I looked around at all the other drivers, assuming they would be just as shocked as I was, and even imagined we would collectively just sit through the next light to process it all. I expected some nice man to jump out of his car and come running to my rescue, asking, "Are you okay?" But, much to my surprise, everyone seemed strangely unaware, as if the entire experience had been visible only to me. How in the world could they have missed what had just happened?

My windshield was shattered and had a hole in it about the size of a golf ball. I immediately thought about the contraband I was carrying in the trunk of my car, pulled over at the first place I found, and with an apology under my breath, discreetly dumped the box in a dumpster behind a liquor store.

I don't think we can ever underestimate the risk we take when we open that gate and allow harmful, destructive people or influences to enter in. I rebelled kind of late and was in my thirties when I made some of the worst choices in my life. I was shocked that lightning didn't strike when I did things that I knew I shouldn't and let people into my life I knew were not good. Honestly, I remember feeling like I had been gypped because I could have been a rule-breaker my whole life if I had known nothing would happen.

But the truth is, lightning doesn't always strike with an immediate bang. Sometimes it comes in little bits and pieces, and even rears its ugly head years later. We must put more value on the gate that we guard for ourselves and for others. In many ways, it is a barrier between life and death, between happiness and torment, or peace and fear. So, when someone or something knocks at that gate, perhaps with great discernment and prayer, our question needs to be "Do you bring light—or do you bring darkness?" It's really that easy. And we shouldn't be afraid to use the key.

> *For you were once darkness, but now you are light in the Lord. Live as children of light (for the fruit of the light consists in all goodness, righteousness and truth) and find out what pleases the Lord. Have nothing to do with the fruitless deeds of darkness, but rather expose them.* (Ephesians 5:8–11)

"IS MOTHER'S DAY COMPLICATED OR WHAT?"

Recently, I heard that the highest volume of calls to addiction crisis hotlines is on Mother's Day. I have not heard a reason why, but looking at the complicated meaning of Mother's Day at Blue Monarch, I have a theory.

Let's face it. Some of the mothers who come to Blue Monarch are not always the ones people want to applaud. After all, they may have lost custody of their children at some point because of something they shouldn't have done. They may have pawned them off on family members or friends so they could pursue what felt more important in that moment—drugs. Their children may have ended up in the foster care system because the state had to step in to take care of them.

Because of this, a huge focus of our program is helping women who have not been very good parents in the past gain the tools to become healthier mothers. And thankfully, through the love and grace of a merciful God, hundreds of children through Blue Monarch have been able to reestablish a relationship with their mothers who had previously lost custody. But how can we possibly celebrate mothers like that?

We often receive tearful calls from concerned mothers who are desperate to find help for their adult daughters. They are very distraught and sometimes just need someone to listen.

But sadly, we also see countless cases where the mother has been perhaps the worst possible influence in a woman's life. We have heard over and over from our residents heartbreaking stories of their mothers prostituting them as young girls in order to support their own drug addictions. We have had a number of women at Blue Monarch who were arrested with their mothers and were even court ordered to have no more communication with them. The mother of one of our residents tried to justify why she had taught her daughter to use meth at the age of fourteen: "Well, if I had known it was her first time, I wouldn't have done it!"

Much of what we see at Blue Monarch is generational drug use and abuse. It is a known fact that a person's social development stops when drug use begins. And since most of our women began using between the ages of eleven and thirteen, this means we see grown women acting like preteens even though they have children of their own. It takes re-parenting to help them grow up and become parents themselves.

The shocking fact, however, is that sometimes their own mothers, and perhaps even grandmothers, began using drugs at the same age. Therefore, their social maturity never developed either. So look what you have—an entire family tree where no one has matured beyond the age of thirteen. Imagine the level of dysfunction, poor choices, and chaos that creates. Just consider what it would take to break that cycle.

For a woman to step out of that vicious familiarity and come to Blue Monarch, where everything is completely new, takes tremendous courage. She may have left behind family members who are angry with her for wanting to get better. In fact, they may even try to sabotage her recovery. After all, when one person gets better, it throws off the dynamics of the entire family.

We had a young woman one time who had been sold for drugs by her own mother as a young girl. When this woman arrived, she easily lost patience with her toddlers and struggled to be a nurturing parent. But something happened in her tenth month here that showed me that terrible cycle had finally been broken.

Her girls were playing with word magnets on the refrigerator door and yelling, "Mommy, Mommy, what is this word? What is this word?" I expected her to get irritated, but much to my surprise, she bent over, carefully examined one of the word magnets in her daughter's hand, and said, "That word is *beautiful* and that's what *you* are." That's when I knew the cycle had been broken, because I suspect that woman had never heard anything like that from her own mother.

The amazing and courageous women we see who take that uncertain step to come out of their homes where everyone uses drugs and bring their children to Blue Monarch, where they can begin a new and completely unfamiliar life, possibly with no family support, are the women I want to salute. They are, without a doubt, the unsung heroes in my eyes.

It's easy to judge women who have not been good to their children. But thank God, when they decide they want to become loving and nurturing mothers, there is a place they can go to learn how. Here.

This month when we focus on mothers, I would like to recognize the brave and remarkable mothers at Blue Monarch. Hold your heads up high. After all, because of your courageous and steadfast determination, your children will now have a chance at the childhood you always wanted. And guess what. So will your grandchildren one day . . . and their children . . . and their children.

That's what I call a happy Mother's Day.

> *Train a child in the way that he should go, and when he is old he will not turn from it.* (Proverbs 22:6 NET)

"WHY IS IT SO FLIPPIN' HARD?"

When my family and I first moved to the Tennessee Cumberland Plateau in 1997, we didn't realize we would be learning an entirely new culture and language, such as "Don't plant your garden until the oak leaf is the size of a squirrel's ear." Good to know.

We loved exploring the nearby areas, traveling down long, curvy roads through the mountains, discovering all kinds of exciting things along the way. But it took a while to learn the customs of the new world we had entered.

For instance, on two different occasions we stopped at interesting yard sales to rummage through the fascinating things on display until we were approached by the homeowners, only to discover nothing was for sale. They were personal treasures that just happened to live in the front yard. "So, so sorry . . . we just thought . . ."

Then there was the morning Clay and I found a new route down the mountain, and we spotted a road sign for a nearby café. Awesome! We loved discovering new places to eat. We traveled down a narrow country road until we found it. Friendly looking place—big, wide porch with rockers and a newspaper stand by the front door.

We parked our car in the gravel lot and entered the café. It was quiet and a little dark inside, but hey, it was early. We seated ourselves at one of the tables and waited for someone to appear. A couple of minutes later, a woman walked in wearing a house robe and slippers and said, "Who are you? What are you doing in here?!"

"We just need to see a menu."

"Well, this isn't a restaurant anymore." *Huh? What about the tables and chairs, and the newspaper stand, and the sign on the road?*

"Hasn't been a restaurant in a long time. We live here now." So we apologized, quickly exited the building, and were grateful we didn't get shot.

How could we be so confused? Honestly, there were days when it seemed we were looking at the world through a distorted mirror at the county fair.

Sometimes I feel like our world at Blue Monarch must seem that way to the women and children we serve. There are many things they may have experienced with their families and friends at home that are not the way we do things here. We have rules about cooking, for instance, like do not pour grease down the drain—or in our neighbor's cow pasture either. We do not allow spanking but encourage other disciplinary options instead. A baby must be held instead of propping up a bottle to feed. The list goes on and on and on.

Even though they are reluctant, it is remarkable that the families we serve agree to change almost every single thing they are accustomed to, let go of the things they learned growing up, and reverse the habits they developed as adults. I often think I would not be able to adapt to so many changes if I were asked to do the same.

Sadly, however, there is one single thing that stands out more than any other, the one thing that is the hardest to change. They believe they can trust no one. This applies to the women *and* the children. The children are just more obvious about it. Sometimes it takes weeks for the children to even make eye contact with our staff members.

This suspicion is so deeply ingrained in them, it takes months and months to prove we can be trusted, and even then, they very cautiously grab onto this concept. They reach out one hand at a time, always keeping one eye open just in case. Consistency is so important in gaining that trust. Just one slipup can be a deal breaker—and then the process starts all over again.

For crying out loud, it's no wonder. Many times, it is the ones they should have been able to trust the most who hurt and violated them the most. How would one ever trust again? They may not have trusted anyone since that first traumatic incident as a child.

I had a young mother sit in my office recently. With tears in her eyes, she confessed that in her seven months with us, she had decided to trust only two people, and even that seemed scary to her. I was honored to be one of the two, but it hurt my heart to think of all the wonderful people she had encountered that she was still keeping at arm's length. She just can't let go of that defense mechanism. The pain it caused her was evident in her face—even in the twisted way she was hugging herself in my chair and wrapping her legs into a knot.

After this woman left my office, I began thinking about all she was missing out on because of her distrust. It made me angry toward all the ones who had hurt her, because they had robbed her of peace and totally changed the lens through which she viewed the world. I considered all the struggles that could have been simpler if she had not been so suspicious of others. The joys she could have experienced if she had just let go of her fears. She was making it so hard. Harder than it had to be.

And suddenly this started to sound familiar . . .

There was a time in our early years when I had a big screaming fit with God. Blue Monarch was a young nonprofit, and money was scarce. I barely had the money to pay the electric bill, and I definitely didn't have enough for payroll the next week. In tears, I bent over my kitchen table, white-knuckled the edge, and yelled, "Why did you ask me to do this if you weren't going to give me the resources to make it happen? What were you thinking?!"

The answer in my spirit came loud and clear. "You are the one who makes it so hard because you don't trust me." This stopped me in my tracks, and I began wondering, *Have I not?* No, I realized I was trying to do Blue Monarch in my own power—not in God's. No wonder it was so flippin' hard!

Since that time, when I get completely overwhelmed and feel like I can't even take a deep breath, I have to remind myself, "Hey, this is God's plan, not yours. Trust him to take care of it, because it's too big for you." And you know what? That always brings immediate relief.

So, Lord, that's the change I so desperately want for this woman.

41

I want her to learn to trust you and the ones you put in her path. I want her to love life—not just survive it. I want her to make up for lost time that was taken by the ones who hurt her. I want her to open up those twisted arms and reach for you. Please speak to her and teach her like you taught me—that it doesn't have to be so flippin' hard. Well, maybe those weren't your exact words, but hey, you know what I mean. Amen.

Update: Turns out my neighbor was right. I should have waited until the oak leaf was the size of a squirrel's ear and my lettuce would not have frozen.

"YOU THOUGHT YOU WERE FINISHED?"

The month of April never comes and goes without my reliving this life-changing and very personal event.

The day was April 24, 2006, and I was driving home from work after a particularly frustrating day. For the three years since we had opened, I had watched numerous women arrive at Blue Monarch, having been addicted to meth, showing absolutely no bond with their children. They interacted with one another as if they were siblings.

I had attended a conference a few years earlier where I'd learned that meth destroys the part of the brain that gives a mother nurturing instincts toward her children. Other parts of the brain can eventually take over this function, in much the same way that a stroke victim's brain may recover, but it takes a long time. Meth was referred to as "the devil's drug," which seemed like a fitting name for something that makes it impossible for a woman to feel love for her own child.

In this conference we watched stunning videos of actual raids on meth labs. Police officers in scary Darth Vader–type masks stormed into houses shouting and pointing guns. What made such an impression on me, though, was that even the smallest, most terrified children did not reach for their mothers. They already knew they were essentially on their own.

On this day back in 2006, I was driving home thinking about how fed up I was with this very issue. I recalled all the women who had left Blue Monarch before they were ready, taking their helpless children with them back into dreadful circumstances, and I was sick of it.

I began to wonder if perhaps my job was done. Maybe my purpose was to get Blue Monarch started and then move on? After watching so many women make terrible choices, I was not even sure we were making a difference. Why bother?

With that thought in my head, I rounded a curve just three miles from my house and could see that an accident had just happened. There was a car upside down and smoking. No other cars seemed to be involved, and there were no emergency vehicles on the scene.

I pulled over to the side of the road, called 911, and began walking to the car. This is where everything began to move in slow motion and every detail became permanently etched into my brain.

My favorite dusty pink leather sandals crunched through the broken glass and gravel as I carefully approached the overturned car. As I got closer, I began to smell a strong odor of alcohol. Well, that's great. A drunk driver. *Look what you've done.*

When I reached the car, I found a woman sitting on the bank with her elbows resting on her bony knees. Her long, dark hair was sloppily piled on top of her head. At first glance she looked very much like all the meth addicts I had seen over the past three years. She was extremely thin and covered in nasty sores, and several teeth were missing. In my present state of mind, I thought to myself, *Another addict! Well, at least you didn't hurt someone else.*

That's when she looked up at me with those dark, empty eyes and calmly said, "Do you think she's going to be okay?"

I looked around and didn't see who she was talking about. But before I could answer, she asked me again, "Do you think she's going to be okay?"

Then, much to my horror, I suddenly discovered a small child, a beautiful little girl, lying in the brush behind her. She was faceup, eyes closed, and I remember thinking how her body appeared to have been carefully placed in the tall weeds and brush even though she had obviously been thrown violently from the car. I rushed to the little girl's side and felt her for a pulse—but she was already gone.

At that moment I felt like I had stepped into hell. Right before my eyes—

in living color—was the very thing I was so sick of. Here was a mother, much like the others I had seen, who was not responding like she had just lost her child, much less due to her own actions. I was so angry with her I could not even look at her.

As this woman stumbled around mumbling to herself about all the trouble she was in, I sat next to her little girl, held her hand, and began praying to God—not to miraculously bring her back, but to thank him for sparing at least one child from a life I could only imagine.

This tragic incident threw me into a deep, dark place. For the first time in my life, I truly understood this thing called "depression." It was frightening to feel something take over my mind that was more powerful than myself, something over which I seemed to have absolutely no control. I had always thought depression was something you just needed to snap out of. It didn't happen to strong people like me. I began to wonder if maybe this was how addiction felt. I remember going to bed praying and pleading, "God, please, let me wake up as someone else—someone who doesn't feel this terrible pain." The world was an ugly place, and surely God was disappointed and disgusted with the entire human race. I was ashamed to be a part of it.

But over the following weeks, God amazingly took this traumatic experience and began speaking to me in powerful and loving ways.

"You have been focusing on all the darkness and not on the light.

"You have forgotten all the children who will not be dead on the side of the road one day—because their mothers came to Blue Monarch.

"You don't know what that mother's life was like that led her to that point—or how different it might have been if she had had a place like Blue Monarch when she needed it." Wow. How true.

And then this: "You thought you were finished? We're just getting started."

That's when the darkness lifted. I realized that indeed, I had been focusing on the disappointments and not celebrating all the victories and miracles I had seen happen over the past three years, which were countless. I had watched women heal from terrible addictions. I had seen mothers develop a bond with their children and become wonderful parents for the first time. Children who had shown up angry and dysfunctional had become healthy, happy kids. But I had focused on nothing but the sadness and disappointment.

This experience ultimately became the beginning of our wonderful Proverbs 22:6 Children's Program. As God said, we *were* just getting started. I became an avid advocate for the children we serve, and our team developed a

Blue Monarch mom loving her daughter

rich program specifically for them. No longer were children just here. They became the focus of our ministry. We realized we had a valuable opportunity to completely change the world of a child, which in turn will change the world of future generations. *"Train a child in the way that he should go, and when he is old, he will not turn from it"* (Proverbs 22:6 NET).

There is a small cross on the side of the road that I see every single day that is a powerful reminder to me of this terrible incident, but there's a photo on my desk that I love. This little girl's father graciously shared a picture of her that I keep where I can always see it. It is a beautiful illustration of how God can take even the most devastating event and turn it into something wonderful. Let's face it. There are hundreds of children who have lived healthier, happier lives and will have much brighter futures because of this special little girl and the impact she had on our ministry.

God was right. It is much nicer focusing on the light. But it's when we bring others into the light with us that it gets even brighter.

"WHAT AM I CALLED IF BOTH MY PARENTS ARE IN PRISON?"

Eight-year-old Justin asked me this question once. He had learned you are called an orphan if both your parents are dead. So he wanted to know what he would be called if both his parents were in prison. His dad was locked up with five more years to serve, and his mother was looking at a possible four years in federal prison, although we were hopeful the judge would allow her to remain at Blue Monarch instead. This painful uncertainty was something Justin and his sister were accustomed to living with daily.

After Justin brought this up, I wasn't able to get this question out of my head. It immediately took me back to a time when I was a child and the kids from the local Children's Home attended my church. A few times I rode back on the bus with them after church to spend the afternoon with some of my friends who lived there.

Today, that same Children's Home has individual homes to provide a more typical family environment, but at that time it was much like a Little Orphan Annie dorm. There was a large, dark brick building with vast rooms, tall ceilings, and cold hardwood floors, and each child had a twin-size bed and chest of drawers filled with only a few belongings lined up against the wall, with numerous children to a room. It never felt cozy or warm. Meals were loud and chaotic in the dining hall, and each child had a chore to complete before leaving the room.

It was common for the children to insist that their moms and dads were coming for them, which rarely happened. And they often gazed out the window as if they expected their parents to drive up at any moment. I wonder now if some of those kids had the same question Justin was asking this day.

I think back on the Justin who first arrived. He was an absolute handful. He was angry and bad about biting those around him. He hit others, including his mom. He yelled *a lot* and was in trouble most of the time. His first week at school started badly when he threatened to kill the father of a classmate. Apparently, it all started when Justin told a little girl she was pretty. Not sure how it escalated so quickly, but in Justin's world this was probably a fairly normal chain of events.

Justin's young journey had already been packed with turmoil. His parents had both been in and out of jail his whole life, he had been moved from place to place numerous times, and he had even been struck by lightning at the tender age of three. Yes, struck by lightning.

But after ten months at Blue Monarch, Justin became a different child. He soaked up life here like a sponge. He absolutely adored his tutor, a gracious man who inspired and motivated him to learn and always took the time to play after their lessons. I can't count the number of times I watched the two of them run past my office on their way to play basketball or toss the football. And Justin's grades? Well, he started the year with only dashes on his report card, but he eventually reached advanced levels in three subjects. As for Justin's behavior? He became proud to run in and report to me that he'd been "green" all day, which meant he had stayed out of trouble at school. It was another miracle.

Justin grew to love the church, his Bible, and the Lord. He once made a card for two of our major donors, and inside the card he asked, "Do you love Jesus?" He drew boxes to mark yes or no. (I suspect they checked yes.) And he gave me this sweet card, which shows he is now a happy boy, despite his uncertain future as his mother's legal issues develop.

One day I held Justin by the shoulders, looked him in the eyes,

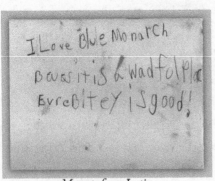

My note from Justin

and said, "Justin, I am *so proud* of you!" He just stood there staring back for the longest time. Then, with big ol' tears in his eyes, he gave me a tight, lingering bear hug and said, "Thank you so much!"

And that's when it hit me. Yes, there actually was a name for Justin if both his parents were in prison. Like all children, either way, he would always be a child of God.

> *So in Christ Jesus you are all children of God through faith.*
> (Galatians 3:26)

"WHAT FORK DO I USE?"

One of my greatest pleasures at Blue Monarch is to introduce our residents to new and exciting experiences. For instance, every year it's a Christmas tradition to take our residents to a "fancy" dinner at a nice restaurant. It is always a very special, memorable evening.

The ride there is almost as fun as the dinner. "What fork do I use?" is one of the most common questions, which usually brings up a reference to Julia Roberts in *Pretty Woman*. One year we clearly didn't get the fork thing figured out, because someone at the table thought it made sense for each person to use a grouping of silverware that included her two forks and her neighbor's knife and spoon. That actually makes sense. As that pattern traveled down the table, it cheated the person at the end, of course. Otherwise, it wasn't a bad idea.

Another time when we wanted to celebrate something special, we got all dressed up and frilly and visited a local tearoom where dainty tea sets were displayed on tables covered in beautiful lacy tablecloths. They treated us to a never-ending supply of wonderful bite-sized sweet and savory treats delivered on three-tiered racks with bottomless cups of hot tea. Some of the women were nervous because they did not want to break or spill anything, and everything within reach looked terribly fragile. Chelsey looked like she was on the verge of hyperventilating, and I could appreciate her pain.

Years ago, when I first met my middle husband, I was invited to Christmas dinner with his family. His world was much different from the one I was accustomed to, so instead of folks wearing their favorite faded jeans for Christmas dinner, the women in his family wore strapless formal gowns and the men wore coats and ties. There was a staff of people in the kitchen who quietly delivered food on silver platters and in crystal bowls to the beautifully laid buffet that sat alongside the elegant dining room table that comfortably seated fourteen.

Since I was a guest, I was invited to be the first in line at the buffet. I was horrified. With no one to watch for guidance, I made my way through the line of food and was delighted to discover something familiar, roast beef and mashed potatoes. Good. I could handle that, although I thought the bowl of mashed potatoes was surprisingly small, which surely meant they were bringing out more in a minute.

I put several slabs of beef on my delicate china plate and topped it with a huge mound of mashed potatoes. Then I made a well, of course, in the middle of the potatoes and filled it with ample gravy. I looked for someone to quickly refill the bowl with more potatoes. Surely they would, since what I'd left would never be enough for everyone else.

Much to my surprise, when I sat down and took a big bite of my potatoes, I immediately discovered it was not mashed potatoes—but horseradish! (Who had heard of such a thing?) Naturally, I was completely mortified, but painfully proceeded to eat the pile of horseradish as if I just happened to love lots of it—with a well full of gravy. My eyes filled with tears, and my sinuses opened up in ways I never knew possible. I could barely catch my breath, and I thought I might die—but I learned a lot that evening and have laughed about this incident for years.

So the other day when I saw Chelsey panic and turn fifty shades of red when she accidentally slurped her soup, when she clinked her cup a little too loudly, and when we thought her asparagus soup might come out her nose when she laughed, it was wonderful. She went into that experience scared to death. But you know what? She enjoyed herself, she learned a lot about proper etiquette, she tasted foods she had never seen before, and she broadened her horizons in the meantime. The world doesn't look the same to her now.

It turns out it is the willingness to step out and try new things—and laugh at yourself in the process—that gives one the courage to take the next step. Chelsey was not the same person when she put down that teacup and walked out the door. She was braver, smarter—and a thousand times more confident. It's all about conquering your fears, even if it's a mountain of horseradish or a cup of hot tea. That's what Blue Monarch is all about.

Returning to old friends and stomping grounds is rarely successful after recovery. We pray that each new and exciting experience makes the old world look less and less appealing.

> *Therefore, if anyone is in Christ, he is a new creation; the old has gone, the new has come!* (2 Corinthians 5:17)

"LET'S TALK ABOUT ABUSE."

I used to think what I saw on television was sensationalized simply to outdo whatever was on the other channels. But sadly, I've learned through my experience at Blue Monarch that the violence on television falls way short of what people really do to one another.

Strangely enough, I have heard more than one firsthand story from a woman who was beaten and then left for dead in a ditch before being discovered days later. Several of our residents have suffered hearing loss or even brain damage from severe blows to the head.

We had one survivor at Blue Monarch who was stabbed seven times and then amazingly lived to tell about it, and another woman who miraculously survived five gunshot wounds to her belly and had to face her attacker in court.

Sometimes I think abuse takes a backseat to addiction. In the beginning of Blue Monarch, I expected to focus primarily on domestic violence, but I quickly learned that drug use becomes the easiest way to self-medicate, and then this often leads to drug addiction. The two go hand in hand much of the time.

Abuse is such a part of the culture in some families, it is not even recognized as abuse. Often our applicants do not consider themselves victims of abuse until they later learn their experience was not normal—or legal. This is especially true if domestic violence was something they observed growing up.

I cannot count the times I have been asked, usually in a sympathetic whisper, if I was motivated to start Blue Monarch because I was a victim of domestic violence. Thankfully, the answer to that question is a big, fat no.

However, someone very dear to me was a victim of abuse, and I struggled for over twenty years to help her find a way out. Somehow there was always an obstacle that prevented her from leaving—and most of those obstacles had to do with one thing: her extremely low self-esteem, which was a hard thing to fix by that time. Surprisingly, one day she made the decision to leave, so we took off to Florida for a few days.

She was like a bird let out of a cage for the first time. She took absolute delight in the simplest things: being able to empty the contents of her purse onto the bed, taking the stairs instead of the elevator, walking barefoot across the room with sandy feet, not having to straighten her naturally curly hair . . . For the first time in many years, she was in control of her life, and she was loving it.

But sadly, this story had a tragic ending. Before our flight back home landed at the airport, her husband violently took his own life, which ended the abuse but did not end the pain, trauma, or damage by a long shot. (I suspect I am not the only one who has pondered "what if" hundreds of times since then.)

We do not exclude men at Blue Monarch. Quite the contrary, we love to have good men volunteer in our program. We have two very smart and wonderful men who lead a book study every Friday with our residents. Faithful male volunteers help by mentoring and tutoring our children or working on maintenance projects. We believe it is important to expose the women and

Madeline and Howell Adams

children to men who are kind, generous, and respectful. In fact, just yesterday one of our residents told me she hoped she could find someone like Daniel one day (a pastor who leads Bible study twice a week) because if she could find someone who loved God the way he did, he would surely love her the right way.

We recently had a lunch to honor Madeline and Howell

Adams, who have completed a significant pledge to Blue Monarch. After every visit we always hear lots of comments about how "down-to-earth and nice" they are. This is so true, but what seems to make the greatest impression on the women of Blue Monarch is how Madeline and Howell express their tremendous love and respect for one another. "Did you see the way she looked at him? Could you believe how sweet he was to her?"

We cover a lot of important issues at Blue Monarch, but through our work to improve self-esteem, build confidence, and study healthy relationships, if we can also raise the bar for future partners, we may have one more chance at changing generations to come.

We want every woman at Blue Monarch to celebrate who she is and realize just how very special God made her. For every day she is reminded of how uniquely wonderful she is, the stronger that conviction becomes embedded in her heart—and the further she gets from allowing someone to convince her otherwise someday.

I praise you because I am fearfully and wonderfully made.
(Psalm 139:14)

"WHAT WERE
YOU THINKING, LORD?"

Sometimes when I hear others talk about their relationship with God, it sounds so beautiful and reverent. But throughout my Blue Monarch journey, there have been many times when my conversations with God have included lines such as "What were you thinking, Lord?!"

One such time was a late night when I was driving down the interstate, returning from Nashville. There I was, minding my own business, listening to music way too loud with the sunroof open. But suddenly, out of the blue, I heard God tell me, "You need to go by Blue Monarch and pray over Kristi."

Well, it was almost 10:30 at night, and there was no way I was doing that. I was not accustomed to walking in the door that late, and certainly not into someone's bedroom. Our residents would think I had lost my mind. And I also convinced myself it would frighten them, and that was reason enough not to go. So there.

"For crying out loud, that's crazy. I'm not doing it." End of story.

As I drove farther down the interstate, I began thinking of Kristi and the struggles she had recently experienced. Over the previous weeks she had lost most of her hearing, and no one could figure out why. It was frustrating for her because she could barely hear, and as a recovering addict in a new place, recently out of jail, healing from a severely abusive marriage, she had enough struggles without that problem too.

As I got closer and closer to the exit I would need to take for Blue Monarch, the message from God just got louder and louder. I could not ignore it no matter how loud I turned up the music. So, as usual, I thought I would cut a deal with God and settle this conflict on my terms.

"Okay, okay, Lord. This is the deal. I will drive out to Blue Monarch—even though it's now almost 11:00 at night. If Kristi's light is on, I'll go in. But if she's in bed, I'm turning around and going home. And by the way, this is crazy, just so you know."

As I drove into the dark driveway at Blue Monarch and made my way to the Woods House, where Kristi was staying, I expected to see a totally dark house. But surprisingly, there was one single light on downstairs. I quietly opened the door and walked inside. And what did I find? Kristi was the only one awake, and she was sitting there, almost as if she expected me.

I sat down next to her and said, "I know this sounds crazy, but God told me to come pray with you." And at that point I could hear God telling me to place my hands over her ears, which I did, even though it felt like a weird thing to do. Then he told me to tell Kristi that it was safe for her to hear now, that she was not going to hear the hurtful things she had heard in the past.

As soon as I told her this, which I had to practically yell, she collapsed and began to weep. And I'm sure you know the rest of the story. Her hearing began returning almost immediately.

Thank you, Lord, for showing me your tremendous power of healing through something I thought was just a crazy idea. And oh, by the way, thank you for being so patient with me for thinking I knew better. What was I thinking?! Amen.

"BUT HE'S OUR BABY."

One of our first residents arrived with a four-month-old baby who had a serious heart condition that had not been treated. The child did not have a healthy, pink glow like most children. In fact, his skin was an odd shade of gray, and he appeared to have gone without a bath for quite some time.

Not too long after this mother and child arrived, the woman left her baby at Blue Monarch and went out of state to reunite with the baby's father. Yes, that's right. She asked us to care for her child and left town with no clear plans to return.

Naturally, I contacted the child's grandmother and assumed she and her husband would immediately rescue their grandchild. But guess what? They did not. They had no intention of solving this mother's problems. They had helped her so many times—they were finished. This is something I understand much better today. But at the time, I was completely confused and disgusted by this reaction.

Therefore, I did what seemed reasonable at the time. I went to court and got temporary custody of the child. I went to work as usual one day—and came home with a baby. I just could not bear the thought of him going to strangers when he had an ordeal like surgery coming up soon.

At this point in our lives, my only child was in college. A baby did not really fit into our world very well, much less one that screamed most nights because of night terrors. Our world was turned upside down, and I did not really have a clear plan for how this might play out. One day at a time.

Soon we began multiple trips back and forth to Vanderbilt Children's Hospital to prepare for heart surgery, and it was difficult to watch his tiny little body go through all that was involved in that process. I have vivid memories of curling up next to him in the hospital crib, desperate to give him a sense of love and comfort during such a frightening time. There was one scary incident when he fought with the oxygen tube until it developed into a middle-of-the-night crisis with a team of nurses and doctors struggling to help him. My heart ached as I had to explain over and over who I was and why his mother was not with him during such a critical time.

There was a young single mom working at Blue Monarch whose lifestyle made much better sense to take on the role of primary care-

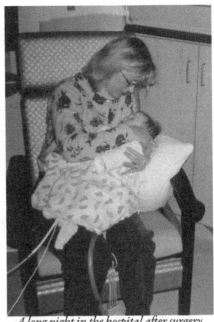

A long night in the hospital after surgery

giver for this baby, but he was still my responsibility, and I loved him. Needless to say, I became extremely attached to this special child and watched him thrive and grow from a sickly four-month-old to a vibrant toddler. He was bright and funny and had a fiery temper. I loved the child and felt a fierce need to protect him. He had a supportive and loving surrogate family surrounding him, and his future looked bright.

But after we had ten months of falling in love with our baby, the grandmother decided she wanted to have him after all. I could not imagine a judge granting her custody when we had become his family, but he did. It was that simple. She was family. We were not.

So, on what appeared to be an ordinary day in a Stuckey's parking lot, we handed him over to the grandmother, along with a list of his favorite foods, which only illustrated how little this grandmother knew about our baby. I felt as if my heart had been ripped out of my chest as I watched them drive away. It was a pain so severe it is impossible to describe.

However, today, all these years later, I thank God for that painful experience. You know why? It is because Blue Monarch is in the business of restoring families. We help women become better parents so they can regain custody of their children. In fact, at this point hundreds of children have reestablished relationships with their mothers who had previously lost custody. But for every child who is reunited with his mother, there is likely a caregiver out there who is left with a broken heart, perhaps watching our car leave the parking lot with the child he or she loves. We may be the ones holding the list of favorite foods.

I know only too well how hard it is to hand your heart to a precious little person, make sacrifices for that child, let your guard down, and dare to imagine a future together, always acutely aware that your time together may be temporary—or may be forever. Either way, you must do the best you can to love this child, without limitations, each and every day, because that's what they need more than anything in that moment.

If not for this personal experience, we might not have encouraged our mothers for all these years to recognize and thank the many foster parents, grandparents, family members, and friends who were willing to care for their children when they were unable to do so themselves.

We rejoice when mothers are able to reunite with their children after lots of hard work and self-improvement. That's a glorious blessing! But we must also appreciate and honor the loving caregivers who are willing to offer their unprotected hearts to a child in crisis. It is possibly God's best way to wrap his arms around his children when they need it the most. And the impact of that special gift is truly immeasurable.

Thank you, Lord, for showing me that in our efforts to reunite mothers and children we must never forget the sacrifices of those who bravely and selflessly step in to fill the gap. Amen.

Update: The grandparents have done a wonderful job of raising this amazing child. He is healthy, happy, extremely bright, and, of course, still adorable.

part two

"YOUR JOB IS TO SERVE, NOT FIX."

In the winter of 2012, I decided I needed a break, and everyone within a fifty-mile radius seemed to agree. I had not been very good at taking time off and still could not allow myself an extended vacation, so I decided to call it a "sabbatical." Yes, that sounded much better. Something productive.

I took off the entire month of January and spent three weeks of that time on the beach with my favorite dog, Lulu—just the two of us—at a surprisingly affordable place right on the ocean. It was perfect. Other than an occasional fisherman, I rarely spotted anyone as far as I could see in either direction. I thought I had landed in heaven.

As soon as I arrived, I felt compelled to make a list of things to accomplish during my sabbatical, which somehow took up an entire page. Next, I explored the beach and collected a bucketful of shells, but immediately dumped them out because it felt excessive. I should limit myself to only one shell a day. What was that about? Clearly, I needed to learn how to relax—and indulge.

Despite my distorted perception of why I was there, this trip quickly became a mountaintop experience for me. I spent most of that time in constant prayer and felt the presence of God in powerful ways that sometimes brought me to tears. There were days when I didn't speak to another living soul other than my husband, so he'd know I was still alive.

One of the things I wanted to accomplish on this trip was to develop a greater love for my Bible. Although I had grown up in the church and as a child could recite the names of the books of the Bible by heart (were those called Bible drills?), I had never really enjoyed my Bible. So I asked God to help me. And, oh my word, did he.

Every morning I jumped out of bed at 5:30 a.m. and rushed out the door to make sure I didn't miss the magnificent sunrise over the ocean. But the strangest thing happened as Lulu and I walked the beach each morning. The numbers of a specific chapter and verse would come to me, again and again, until I hurried back and anxiously grabbed my Bible to see what it said. Never did it take me to the middle of a sentence or to a "so-and-so begat so-and-so." It always related to exactly what was on my heart that day.

The first morning this happened, I was walking the beach feeling a little guilty for taking so much time off when suddenly "Ecclesiastes 3" jumped into my head for no reason. It seemed like such a random book of the Bible, so out of curiosity I looked it up when I got back to the house. It was the passage about how there is a time for everything, which I interpreted to include taking time off. After this I tore up my list of "Things to Accomplish on My Sabbatical" and gave myself permission to keep, without shame, every last shell I found the least bit fascinating.

The next morning, I walked the beach feeling weary and downright exhausted from carrying the load of hundreds of women and children for whom I had felt responsible over the past nine years. There were many times when it no longer felt like a joy and privilege but an enormous burden, especially when things didn't turn out the way I thought they should.

Out of nowhere, "Numbers 11:11–15" popped into my head, and I thought it had to be a mistake. Wasn't the book of Numbers all about numbers? Surely, either I had heard God wrong or perhaps he had accidentally given me the wrong verse. "Don't you mean one of the other books that start with *N*?"

Much to my surprise, Numbers 11:11–15 showed me that Moses had felt just as burdened, frustrated, and overwhelmed as I did. Wow! That was so comforting. Turned out God had the verses right all along, and I felt like he was telling me, "It's okay that you feel this way."

I know I am not the only one who has had this kind of experience. But it was such a special time for me, spending this one-on-one time with Jesus each day. Since then, this temporary sanctuary turned into my "happy place," and my mind goes back to that time on the beach at the most unexpected moments.

Toward the end of my sabbatical, as I felt stronger and healthier, I asked God to show me how I might avoid getting so exhausted again. How could I protect my staff from reaching that point as well? This time the answer came in a clear and powerful directive that forever changed the course of how we operate at Blue Monarch.

"Your job is to serve, not fix. To love, not judge."

This got my attention. I began thinking back on some of the most exhausting ordeals we had experienced at Blue Monarch, and in every single incident we were indeed trying to fix someone, and perhaps even judging them, which was hard to admit. I realized that by starting each day trying to fix people, we were bound to end the day feeling we had failed, because we cannot fix people. But God can. No wonder I was so exhausted. I was trying to do God's job.

I also saw that by starting each day with the goal to serve, we would end every single day knowing that yes, we had indeed served the women and children of Blue Monarch that day. And served them well.

I brought this message back to our staff, and since then, when we find ourselves overwhelmed and defeated, we ask ourselves, "Wait. Are we trying to serve this person? Or are we trying to fix this person?" This usually puts everything into perspective.

We would all rather fix. By fixing we get to be in charge and determine what's best for someone. But by simply serving, the outcome may fall way short of what we want, and our hearts may get broken in the process.

This is never clearer than when we lose a resident before she has accomplished all we had in mind for her. We want her to drive out with an exciting job in place, a new home in a wonderful neighborhood, and happy children by her side. However, sometimes as we watch them drive off, even though it is painful, we must accept that by serving them we may have stopped the madness for a while in a safe and loving home, and they may have avoided a disaster only God knows about. We may have nurtured seeds that otherwise might never have been planted.

In other words, what I have come to realize is this:

God may first need us to serve and love—before the fixing can truly begin.

"WILL IT BITE?"

I'll jump at a sudden noise, but it takes a lot to really scare me. However, I vividly remember a day when I had a rush of fear I have never forgotten.

My husband and I live near a magnificent waterfall that belongs to the state of Tennessee. When we first moved to the mountain over twenty years ago, we loved walking to the base of the falls, which is a long, steep trail down a couple hundred feet. A swinging bridge takes you to a beautiful pool of water with massive boulders, and after a big rain, the roar of the falls is deafening.

One Tuesday morning I decided to hike to the falls by myself. My dog Lady followed me, and off we went. I typically enjoyed the park more during the week than on weekends because there were no hikers or rock climbers and I could have the place to myself.

Halfway down the steep, rugged descent to the base of the falls, I suddenly looked up and found five filthy, rough-looking grown men standing there. They did not look like rock climbers—that was for sure. And they did not look like typical hikers either. They seemed terribly out of place.

"Well, look, fellas, there's a lady in the house." Their reactions were hard to read.

My heart stopped. Oh man, this was such a stupid thing for me to do—taking this hike without telling anyone where I was going. By the way the hair on the back of my neck stood up, I knew this did not feel right. It occurred to me that if I ran, their instincts might be to chase me, even if they had not planned to. So I decided I needed to make them believe I had absolutely no reason to be afraid. I continued walking straight toward them on the trail, even though it was the exact opposite of what I really wanted to do. I hoped they would assume I had a whole brigade of burly men following me who might appear at any moment. (This was way before we had cell service in the area.)

Much to my surprise, when I got face to face with the five men, every one of them suddenly sat down on the ground at the exact same time. I didn't know what it meant or what was about to happen.

"Will it bite?!" they asked. I couldn't understand what they were talking about, because Lady unfortunately had run on without me and was no help. Thanks a lot, Lady.

"Will what bite?" I asked.

"*That!* Will it bite?!" They all pointed to the top of the ridge and looked like they were completely terrified. Much to my surprise, my dog Missy was standing there—but even though she was a chow mix with one eye, she had never looked the least bit threatening, so I could not understand the men's extreme reaction to her. She was a sweet dog and had never bitten anyone.

Nevertheless, since they seemed to think she was dangerous, I said, "Well, that's the thing. You just never know."

Missy had never made this hike with me before and never did again after this day, but she quickly ran down the mountain and stood next to me until all five men got up and hurriedly scrambled up the trail out of sight.

I have always believed that God caused them to see something much scarier than my harmless dog Missy. There is really no other explanation for their bizarre behavior. Those rough and tough men were clearly scared to death for no apparent reason.

But I will admit, I was terrified of what could have happened that day, and I have remembered this event many times since then. However, I was an adult when this happened, and I also understood that I had gotten myself into this predicament through my own poor judgment.

On the other hand, we often have little children at Blue Monarch who have had much more terrifying and traumatic experiences, much scarier than mine, at the hands of others and through no fault of their own. Many of our children have hidden for safety in places you and I would think are pretty creepy—like the dark crawlspace of a house. We had a young boy who had a history of hiding under his house until he heard his mother sing their special song to let him know it was safe to crawl out.

We had a sweet little boy living with us once who had good reason to be terrified of dogs. When this child was only two, someone he should have been able to trust allowed a pit bull to lunge at him over and over, only to yank the dog back when it was within a few inches of his face. The man did this for his own amusement, but it caused this little boy to develop a terrifying and severe fear of dogs. Even puppies made him hysterical.

This is a great example of the individual nature of our ministry. It is not in our curriculum to help a child overcome the fear of dogs. But once we learned of this child's history and why he was so frightened of our farm animals, and dogs in particular, we wanted to help him overcome this terrible fear, and in the process, learn to trust others.

Well, I am happy to report that after we worked with this child to heal his fear of dogs, his mother was moved to tears because he was finally able to overcome this tremendous fear and even love on a dog and enjoy playing with her. What a triumph! The smile on his face was priceless.

The mother's explanation was that this peaceful place, and her son's new sense of security here, allowed him to overcome not only his fear of dogs but his fear of all animals, and even the dark. He no longer insists on keeping a light on at bedtime. She said, "All his fear has been removed because we are at Blue Monarch."

When someone asks, "How do you measure success?" I will not think of spreadsheets and statistics. I will think of this frightened, angry child who stomped through our doors just months ago—and the loving, happy child who left us, no longer tortured and fearful. And I will be reminded of the mother who regained custody of her son and loved him so much, she desperately wanted him to be healed of his debilitating fear and was moved to tears when it happened. I will also think of the amazing way God led them both to Blue Monarch, a place where they could find the help they so desperately needed.

So how do we measure success? By observing stories like this one every single day.

> *So do not fear, for I am with you; do not be dismayed, for I am your God.* (Isaiah 41:10)

"IS THIS MY OWN NERVOUS BREAKDOWN?"

I did not reach my fundraising goal for the year 2016. In prior years, this would have put me into quite a state of panic. However, I had a sense of peace about the unexpected shortfall and continued to pray for abundance. For many years I foolishly prayed for only what we needed, but in 2016 as a staff we shifted all our prayers to those of abundance—not necessarily monetary abundance, but abundant blessings.

Before the end of the year, I had a significant dream in which God showed me the campus of Blue Monarch from the air. He lifted off something like a lid, and when he did, magnificent bright light burst out of it and filled the sky. I felt he was telling me not to worry, that 2016 was going to be a great year and, in my own words, "bust wide open!" Boy, was he ever right.

In another dream, I once again saw our campus from the air, and in the area of our property that used to be a landing strip for the previous owners, I saw a plane land behind the trees and four helicopters rise into the air. I had no interpretation for that one—at least not yet.

Weeks later, on an otherwise ordinary Friday afternoon in February, I checked my email before I left my office for the weekend. I was excited to see that I had a message from one of my favorite donors, Bob, who was living in New Hampshire with his wife, Jacque. Or so I thought.

Bob informed me that Jacque had passed away, which I was disappointed and sad to hear. "Jacque was a wonderful, loving wife, mother of four great children, grandmother to nine up-and-coming young people, plus three great-grandchildren. Naturally, we, her family, would like to honor her memory in some meaningful way. One compelling idea is to do something in conjunction with Blue Monarch, to which she felt an immediate connection since we first learned about your efforts to help mothers and their children get out of the clutches of abuse and addiction and back into mainstream society."

Bob went on to describe how he and his children wanted to dedicate a playground to her since she had cared so much about physical fitness. I thought this was an awesome idea. He had me at this point, because I was so excited to honor her in this way. Yay! A new playground! What a great way to end the week.

But then in the last paragraph, Bob went on to describe how he and his four children wanted to donate a "good portion of Jacque's estate" to Blue Monarch. And he put the dollar amount in parentheses.

Okay—this is a moment I will never forget. In fact, this goes right up there with the day a man walked on the moon. My first thought was that my imagination was running completely amok. I remembered as a child hearing about a neighbor who'd had a "nervous breakdown," and since it had happened to her in the grocery store, I assumed it was this uncontrollable thing that could happen to you at any moment—at any place. Was this my own nervous breakdown? Was I imagining things?

I sat there and stared at the number. I counted the zeros several times. And this was the amazing thing. No matter how I moved the commas around, it was still incredible.

For fear this wasn't really going to happen, I was hesitant to share the news with anyone other than a few close family members and friends. But most had the same reaction. Tears. Immediate tears. Yes, it was overwhelming news for sure, and I often wondered if I was simply walking around in some sort of altered state.

A few weeks later I met with Bob and two of his four children. We discussed some ideas as to how this gift might be used and how it could fit into the future plans we already had in place. One of the ideas that appealed to them the most was one that was on my own personal bucket list: building four cottages for our graduate transitional program. This program has been hugely successful in preparing our graduates for the outside world in a supportive environment, but we had only one cottage for this purpose. We call the program WINGS, which stands for Women in Newly Grounded Success.

I was especially excited because all three of them agreed that if we were going to do something, why do it in an ordinary way? Let's make the cottages extraordinary. We already had a reputation for providing a uniquely beautiful home for a population that often finds help in more institutional facilities. We, however, have a former bed-and-breakfast on a beautiful fifty-acre farm, and the cottages needed to live up to that standard.

We all agreed that the perfect location for the cottages was in the beautiful field that used to be a landing strip. It was particularly fitting since Bob was a pilot. Interesting, huh? And they have four children? Four helicopters? Four cottages?!

Our first four WINGS cottages
Rendering by Hannah Goodgion with Hodgson Douglas

We also discussed using the other half of this gift to establish an interest-bearing account for Blue Monarch to use for major projects and sustainability. This would be the first time in the history of our organization that we had such a fund.

Bob then asked if I would plan Jacque's memorial service and incorporate a groundbreaking ceremony as well. I could not have been more honored. And it was especially moving that this memorial service would take place on our own Blue Monarch campus.

In a private ceremony, we had this special day. Family members gathered from across the country. We celebrated the amazing woman Jacque was—an adventurer, a world traveler, an avid athlete, an amazing mother and wife. We marveled at how many parallels there were between what she stood for, how she raised her children, and what we do at Blue Monarch. It was no wonder she was so drawn to Blue Monarch. Bob said after her first visit she came home talking about us and kept talking about Blue Monarch for days after.

We laughed at the remarkable way Jacque first learned about Blue Monarch—through her bowling buddy, Pat. That was back when they still lived in Tennessee. And we absorbed the deep meaning of how this gift, which originated from Bob and Jacque but is being granted by their four children, not only demonstrates the continuation of her generous heart through her family members but will also impact so many women and children in the years to come.

The four siblings each had beautiful brass plaques designed that feature their own personal sentiments about their mother, along with words of encouragement for the families who will live in the cottages. Our upcoming graduates and their children, who would be the first to live in the cottages, participated in a special ceremony celebrating the life of Jacque.

It was a glorious day. And it was truly a day of abundance—not just abundance in gifts, but abundance in new friendships, abundance in community support, abundance in the numbers of women and children we will be able to serve, and abundance in the blessings they will receive.

In looking back, I have to wonder, how many times are we praying for a Pinto when God really wants to give us a Cadillac? The Bible is filled with examples of how much he loves us and wants to give to us abundantly. But it is also filled with instruction that we must first ask—and also believe we will receive.

> So I say to you: *Ask and it will be given to you; seek and you will find; knock and the door will be opened to you. For every-*

one who asks receives; the one who seeks finds; and to the one who knocks, the door will be opened. Which of you fathers, if your son asks for a fish, will give him a snake instead? Or if he asks for an egg, will give him a scorpion? If you then, though you are evil, know how to give good gifts to your children, how much more will your Father in heaven give the Holy Spirit to those who ask him! (Luke 11:9–13)

"WELCOME,
THE BETTY CROCKER OF METH."

Laurie was the very first resident at Blue Monarch—and our first graduate. Laurie loved to boast, "There will never, ever be another *first* graduate of Blue Monarch!" And she was so right.

The news of Laurie's recent death from a heart attack hit me harder than I would have expected, and I believe it is because Laurie was symbolic of so many "firsts" in this Blue Monarch journey. I had the great honor of speaking at her memorial service, and this allowed me to really examine how deeply Laurie impacted my life.

When we first got our beautiful property in 2003, I received a frantic call from a mother of four children. She was desperately looking for help. At the time, I was trying to run Blue Monarch as I would any other business and could not see a way to help her until we had our staff and program completely in place. So I turned her away.

However, for two weeks this mother stayed on my mind. I finally tried to track her down and discovered that within those two weeks this woman had surrendered all four children to others who were willing to adopt them—and she had then disappeared. My heart was broken.

I realized in that moment that life-changing events happened very quickly for the population we were going to serve—so the next woman who called was not getting turned down, no matter how unprepared we might be.

That next woman was Laurie, known as the "Betty Crocker of Meth" to some, and this reputation had landed her in jail. She had been released and was looking for a new start.

I have a photo of her interview at Blue Monarch, and in looking back I have to wonder if I was making up the questions as I went along. I'm not sure. What I do remember, though, is that I had never heard such tragic stories in my entire life. One story I have already mentioned was of her being left in a ditch to die for several days after being severely beaten. There were lots of other disturbing stories—one right after the other. I immediately realized I was in way over my head, but yes, we were taking her anyway.

The day Laurie moved in, I watched her from my office window as she strolled the beautiful grounds admiring her new home. I got an immediate rush of *Oh my word! I am responsible for this person! What have I done?*

I keep a photo of this moment on my desk because God quickly pointed out to me, "This is my plan. Not yours." And I have discovered the world is much less scary when I remember this very important fact.

Truth was, even though Laurie came to Blue Monarch for help, and it was exactly what she needed at that point in her life, God also knew I desperately needed a teacher. I knew absolutely nothing about the population our organization was designed to serve, and I am sure Laurie figured that out

Laurie checking out her new home

right away. I had a fine arts degree, for crying out loud.

What I learned from Laurie, though, became the very foundation of what we do and helped to shape what we have become.

Here are just a few of the valuable things Laurie taught me:

- The world of drug abuse and what it does to destroy families—and especially how it impacts the children in the midst of the chaos.
- Not to make eye contact with people who are currently using meth, so I don't get caught up in their crazy paranoia.
- The world of crime and law enforcement—how to work with probation officers and judges, and how to navigate a jail interview.

- The different kinds of physical, sexual, and verbal abuse and how they cause severe damage to one's emotional health and self-worth.
- How to protect myself from people who are manipulative, and to have greater discernment regarding the people around me. In other words, she taught me "street smarts" that have really come in handy through the years.
- What happens when harmful, destructive cycles of behavior are allowed to continue generation after generation.

I watched Laurie grieve the hideous, suspicious deaths of her mother and little brother, which taught me how injustice comes in all shapes and sizes for some, but not for others.

But while I observed Laurie's steadfast courage and determination as she recovered from a life of abuse and addiction, she also taught me volumes about forgiveness, emotional healing, and most importantly, faith in God. Her love of Christ was tangible, and she gave him the glory for her healing.

I have always thought one of life's greatest tragedies would be to get to the end of your life, look back, and see that you haven't accomplished anything significant. That is certainly not true for Laurie.

Laurie raised two amazing children, Robbie and Becca. Thankfully, they have not repeated the cycle of drug abuse in their family and are both vibrant, successful young adults. Laurie has a beautiful granddaughter who only knew her grandmother as completely wonderful. Laurie was a devoted daughter and even restored her relationship with her father while she was at Blue Monarch.

But this is what Laurie probably never knew: She impacted the lives of hundreds of women who followed in her footsteps. She paved the way for many, many women who showed up on our doorstep with the same hurts, disappointments, and tragedies that she experienced. But because of Laurie, we were better equipped to help them.

Through the years, our residents have asked me many times, "How is your first graduate doing?" They ask as if they are afraid to hear the answer.

I have always been very proud to say that our first graduate was successful and doing well. Then I show them the photo on my desk of the day Laurie graduated from our program. Laurie always said, "Miss Susan, the Holy Spirit must have been with us in this photo, because just look at the incredible glow!" I would have to agree. It was an amazing, triumphant day—not just for Laurie, but also for the Kingdom of God.

As I visited with Robbie and Becca at Laurie's memorial service, it was moving to discover the tremendous impact Blue Monarch had on their lives, even though the time Laurie was with us was very brief in her life of fifty years.

Robbie shared, "Mom's time at your program was the first time she was able to be a real mom. Even though I was entering college at the time, it was the first time she was ever involved in my school."

One time many years ago, Laurie told

Laurie and me soaked in the light of the Holy Spirit

me that if it weren't for Blue Monarch, she would probably be dead. At the time, I thought she was being a little dramatic. But last week Becca told me, "If it weren't for Blue Monarch, we wouldn't have had all these extra years with Momma. So thank you for what you do for families."

And then Robbie said, "If it weren't for Blue Monarch, I don't think our mom would have made it another year."

Guess Laurie was not exaggerating after all.

> *Thank you, Lord, for taking the darkness of Laurie's life and using it to bring light to so many. And thank you for sending the perfect teacher to partner with me on this amazing journey. Amen.*

"WELL, THEN I WILL BE THE FIRST."

Surely, it was a sick April Fool's joke. It was the evening of April 1, 2017, when I got a text from one of our Blue Monarch graduates. She forwarded me a Facebook post with Emily's beautiful face that indicated she had died that day—April Fool's Day. We were hoping it wasn't true.

But it was true.

Just two days later would mark a year since Emily had graduated from our program. My mind immediately flashed back to her bubbly personality, great sense of humor, and sparkling blue eyes. And then, of course, to her adorable children.

Emily was so full of life, I could not help but remember some of her funny moments—like the time we all went to a local tearoom for high tea. She surprised us by breaking into a perfect English accent as soon as we walked in the door, and she stayed in character the entire time we were there, which kept us in stitches. How could she be gone?

When my father died, I described that painful journey as a train ride where you stop at depots along the way and exchange one suitcase of grief for a different suitcase of grief. It seemed there were distinctly unique stages of grief that came in all shapes and sizes.

The first suitcase I grabbed when Emily died was one of complete shock. I spent the next twenty-four hours basically numb as I systematically called each staff member to break the terrible news. I wanted to cry, but for some reason I could not.

The next day was Monday, and the suitcase I carried that day was one of making sure everyone on our staff had oxygen. I had two psychologists who are very dear to us meet with our staff to help process what had happened. Some of us had spent eighteen months living very closely with Emily, and a few new ones on our team only knew her by name. But it was immediately clear that her death had impacted each of us in powerful and personal ways, and we were all hurting terribly for the children left behind.

I will have to admit, as I looked around the room at the amazing people on our staff and observed how they were hurting so deeply over Emily's death, I had to resist having a few George Bailey moments where I wondered if all these people could have been spared this pain if I had not started Blue Monarch in the first place. And yes, I do realize how crazy that is, but it was hard not to feel some ownership in the raw hurt I saw around me that day.

The third day I held in my hands a suitcase of great anger. I kept thinking back on the day Emily had sat in my office and announced she was not going to participate in our transitional graduate program, but instead she was going home to take care of her mother and brother, who needed her. Someone had given her mother enough money to turn the electricity back on in Emily's house. That was all it took to spring her back like a bungee cord to the worst place she could possibly go. (Emily's mother and brother are now incarcerated, so the sheriff's department escorted them both to the funeral home.)

"Emily, I'm telling you. Please listen to me. I have sat here with many women through the years who also wanted to return to their old environments, and not one of them was successful doing that. Not one."

I will never forget. In that tiny baby voice of hers, with a smile of confidence on her face, Emily leaned back in her chair and said, "Well, then I will be the first."

Emily was the first, but not for that. Even though I cannot stand to hear condolences that begin with "At least . . . ," I found myself trying to get some kind of comfort in the fact that *at least* she was the first we had lost due to drug-related circumstances, which was remarkable considering we had served hundreds of women struggling with addiction. However, this staggering statistic brought absolutely no comfort and felt quite empty.

My next suitcase held great sorrow. It was the heaviest suitcase so far, and I am still holding it today, although it is slowly getting lighter. In fact, it took a while before I realized I had gone an entire day without unexpectedly bursting into tears—the kind where you find a quiet place to cry out loud. Emily's tragic death at the young age of twenty-three, and the impact it will have on her children, had a profound effect on me.

A while ago, well before I knew anything like this was on the horizon, I got an unexpected email from a professor at a Texas university. Unbeknownst to me, she had been using Blue Monarch for several years as an example of a nonprofit doing recovery right. She asked if I would speak to her class of seniors who were going into the field of recovery. We planned to do this online, and I began keeping a list of "Ten Things I Wish I Had Known," which quickly turned into twenty.

All of a sudden one weekend, I felt God telling me, "You need to go there in person. You need to be there." I had never been to that area of Texas, and when I looked online to see if it was obvious why God would want to send me there, I can't say anything jumped out at me. But I contacted the professor and said, "If it's all the same to you, I think I will come speak to your class in person." She seemed very excited, and as soon as I made my travel arrangements, I felt great peace about my decision.

After Emily's death, however, I realized my trip to Texas was going to conflict with her memorial service. Maybe I needed to reschedule or cancel my trip.

Suddenly it became clear to me why I needed to go. I had the opportunity to talk to a roomful of compassionate people who were going into the field of recovery. What better way to honor Emily's life than to empower people who were joining our army to fight the ugly world of addiction!

With a heavy heart, as Emily's memorial was taking place back at home, I made sure the students in front of me would know how to spell Emily's name and remember her face. I wanted them to know that the people they will serve one day are very real. I described Emily's life and the trials she experienced as a young child, finding herself as the primary caregiver for her younger brother at the age of eight. I shared Emily's childhood stories of how desperately she longed for her parents to do the ordinary things other parents did—and I told of how she learned to do those things for her own children while she was at Blue Monarch.

I showed the class the staggering chart Emily made in one of our classes that illustrated how multiple people on one side of her family tree had died from suicide, and multiple people on the other side had been murdered. Sadly, even the autopsy would not tell us on which side of the tree Emily's death belonged.

I described how Emily arrived at Blue Monarch without custody of her children. And then I shared the beautiful memories she made with them when they were reunited and how much their relationships grew during such an impressionable time in their young lives. I talked about the rich experience her little ones had as they were able to grow and thrive in a healthy environment and Christian home. How our farm provided a place for her children to just be kids instead of worrying about grown-up problems at such a tender age.

Then I felt compelled to share with the class one of the most important lessons God has taught me—that our job is to serve, not fix. Love, not judge. It was important for them to know that the services they provide may have an impact down the road, one they may never see. I knew there would come a time when these students would question whether they were really making a difference in the ugly world of addiction.

And there it was. That right there was why the last suitcase was so heavy. How do we experience something like this without questioning whether we are really making a difference? I found myself asking this question over and over as I grasped for answers. However, I got the answers to my own question from Emily herself.

One day, while going through a box of similar letters from previous residents, I found the ones from Emily that described how much she had gained at Blue Monarch, and all the reasons she wished she had not left when she did—especially since she quickly landed herself in jail. Over and over, she described the relationship with Jesus she had developed while she was here. She even drew me a picture of Jesus. "I'm not much of an artist, but this is my first time ever trying to draw Jesus. I'd like you to have it." So there it was. The greatest blessing of all was the change in Emily's heart.

Emily's drawing of Jesus

Still, I read through all Emily's letters to see if there was anything else that would help me feel we had made a lasting difference. And then I found one more thing…

From a jail cell Emily had written, "When I spoke to my son, you know what he wanted to talk about? Normally it's always been 'Mommy, why you in jail? Why was you bad? When you coming back?'—all bad things, but he didn't ask any of that. The only thing he said was 'Mommy, I want to go back to Blue Monarch.'"

Sometimes I feel the biggest challenge we face in what we do is not even the drugs. It is the extremely intense pull of what is familiar. It is typically what they knew as children. So, even though it may be dysfunctional, chaotic, and even harmful, they are naturally drawn to it like a magnet. Therefore, we want to become *that*. We want to become that same powerful, pulling force for the children we serve.

We want the life we provide at Blue Monarch to be what our children spring back to like a bungee cord. We want to be what is familiar to them, what they long for even as adults. For Emily, even though her story did not turn out the way we wanted, she gave her children a beautiful gift by providing them wonderful memories of a life they might have otherwise never been exposed to, and one she never had as a child. A place where the world is safe, people are nurtured and loved, and the future is bright and full of hope. Emily planted those seeds in her children, and we must pray they will continue to grow.

A few weeks after I spoke in Texas, I got a special package in the mail. It was filled with lots of nice notes from the students. My goal was for just one student to make a difference in someone's life because of Emily's story. But after reading what some of them had to say, I can see that Emily planted many seeds there too—way over in West Texas.

Thank you, Emily, for sharing your life—and death—with us, because I believe God found a way to turn your darkness into light for many others. And that's a suitcase I'm honored to carry for a long, long time.

"BON APPÉTIT."

It started out so lovely. There we were, eating lunch side by side. The sweet toddler in the highchair next to me was slurping chicken noodle soup while I enjoyed my leftover kale soup. Swimming lessons had just ended, and we were at the Blue Monarch kitchen table as moms, kids, and staff members scurried around preparing their lunches. The room was filled with lots of laughter and chatter. That is one of the things I love about bringing my lunch. It gives me a chance to visit with the women and children we serve and get to know them better. It was another special Blue Monarch moment.

Then—with no warning—I heard a loud splashing sound, almost with the force of a fire hydrant. Turned out, the adorable little girl next to me was calmly spooning noodles into her mouth, all the while peeing a river through her swimsuit, right onto the hardwood floor. She must have a bladder the size of a watermelon, because there was a virtual pond beneath her chair.

I guess this is a great example of the environment in which we work, because I paused to say "Bon appétit" to no one in particular, informed her mother that we had guests coming any minute and it would be nice if the massive mess on the floor was gone, then kept eating my soup as if nothing had happened. (It is not always a Hallmark moment at Blue Monarch with hosts of angels singing in the background.)

When I was a young teenager, I made frequent visits to the doctor's office for a nagging stomach problem. In looking back, I think I was simply anxious about being a teenager. But I grew very tired of the routine, which always began with a pesky urine sample.

One morning before my mother and I left for yet another doctor's appointment, I happened to look in the refrigerator and discover a Tupperware container filled with leftover pineapple juice—the really syrupy kind from a can of pineapple rings. *Hey! That looks familiar.* So I decided to play a little joke. This was going to be great.

I hid the plastic container in my purse and could hardly wait to implement my brilliant plan. Sure enough, as soon as my name was called, the nurse handed me the usual cup and nodded toward the bathroom. Just in case someone was listening, I turned on the faucet and let it run while I carefully poured the pineapple juice into the cup and flushed the excess down the toilet. I marched out the door and placed the cup on my file folder as I had been instructed, then took my seat to watch what would happen next, which I had not considered until that moment.

I could hardly contain myself. This was completely hilarious and, without a doubt, one of the best tricks I had ever played. It was hard to keep a straight face while I watched the nurse run her test on my fake urine specimen. She quickly ran another one. Then another one. Her face gradually turned white as a sheet, and she became increasingly frantic.

Suddenly she jumped up, grabbed the two doctors in the hallway, and rushed them back to see the results. They looked just as alarmed as she did. Occasionally they glanced over their shoulders at my innocent mother in the waiting room, then turned their backs and frantically whispered among themselves.

Eventually the nurse looked over at me, and I guess I must have looked guilty because she yelled, "WHAT IS THIS?!"

Immediately I realized my joke was not funny to anyone but me. I confessed it was pineapple juice. Apparently, the sugar level was sky high, and no one was laughing. Especially my mother.

Both doctors stomped off in total disgust. The nurse just stood there shaking her head as the color in her face swung all the way back to beet red. No doubt they grumbled to themselves, "We come to work every single day only trying to help people—and then she comes in here expecting us to fix her problem when she's not willing to do her part!"

Does that sound familiar?

We do random drug testing at Blue Monarch. In fact, we test for a variety of things: drugs, alcohol, and even nicotine. (We are a nonsmoking facility.) Occasionally, we have someone who tries to fool us and finds ways to fake a test. Instant coffee, her child's urine stored in a water bottle, you name it and someone has tried it.

This always irritates me. A woman comes to us for help, we are committed to helping her change her life, and then she does something like this that only cheats herself. Are we not all on the same team here? Team Help Her?

In fact, we may not be. At least not yet. Many of our women arrive here very broken. Some have developed sharp survival skills that may show up as deceit, manipulation, and even ugly entitlement. Often, they do not trust us—and they are suspicious of anyone who wants to help. "Why are you doing this for me?" which usually means "What's in it for you?"

These are thick, heavy walls to tear down. It takes lots of time, great patience, loads of prayer, pretty intensive work—and especially the tremendous grace and mercy of God to reach that sweet place of redemption. But in the meantime, there are some days when I honestly want to grab a woman by the shoulders and say, "What were you thinking? Don't you see we are only trying to help you? Do we care more about your recovery than you do?!"

That's when I have to take a deep breath and ask God to please show me what he sees in her. "Please, Lord, please help me see her through your eyes, because I'm having a hard time loving her today." And each time I get the same response.

"She is my daughter. And I love her."

Well, this does the trick every time. In that moment I am humbly reminded that she and I are actually sisters. We are both children of God, and he loves each of us the very same—even on the days she hands us pineapple juice.

Thank you, Lord, for the raw and beautiful reality of recovery that you so graciously allow us to witness day after day. Help us to feel your presence, even on the days that are hard. Thank you for the gentle reminders that we are always to love others as you love us, and that when we do, the results can be amazing. Amen.

"I AM PROUD OF MYSELF!"

One of our mothers had to be discharged from our program. She had blatantly broken some of our rules, was not putting forth the effort she should, and made this decision unavoidable for us. It is always hard to see a woman leave when we feel she is capable of so much more, but when she takes her innocent children with her, it becomes even more painful. In fact, this may be the toughest part of our job.

Right before they left, the oldest child, a spunky little girl, came into my office to give me a hug. I hugged her back, once again choking back the tears, knowing I would probably never see her again. Before she walked out the door, I quickly said, "I'm proud of you!" And I have not gotten the next moment out of my head since that day.

This young, brave girl immediately straightened her back, held her head high, looked straight ahead, and said, "I am proud of myself!" Then she walked out the door as if marching into battle. She reminded me of a character in a Normal Rockwell painting.

I realized in that moment that she had already begun shifting back into the role of the parent. She knew her mother had messed up, she realized their lives were returning to chaos, and she was already positioning herself to take care of her siblings as she had done before they came to Blue Monarch.

There is a subtle melody that plays every day at Blue Monarch, and even though the tune never ends, it goes relatively unnoticed. I think of it as our own "Rhapsody in Blue." Sometimes the music is peaceful or playful. Other times it is loud and almost a little dark. But it is the ebb and flow and fluid interaction between treble and bass that remind me so much of what happens with our mothers and children as they fight to find their proper places as parent and child.

Things are often very disjointed and dysfunctional when our families show up at the door. The mother may have never had a healthy childhood, and she is hanging on to the hope that she will still get one somehow. Therefore, she is acting like a child even though she has several children of her own.

Then, the oldest child shows up as the parent. He has taken care of his siblings for a long time, has worked to keep his mother in line the best he can, and is accustomed to solving grown-up problems way beyond his years. Our children often arrive overly concerned about things no child should have to worry about—like shelter and food. They sometimes hoard food because they have learned this as a way to survive.

We had a young girl for a while who got off the school bus every day and came straight to my office with her list of things to discuss. It was amusing, but also a little sad. The list usually consisted of things she should never worry about—a leak in the tub upstairs . . . the backpack she wanted me to remind her mother about . . . her concern over her mother's struggles to quit smoking.

So we had a problem. The mother was the child, and the child was the parent. However, the mother had chosen to come to Blue Monarch because she desperately wanted to become the parent, a healthy mother. This dramatic switch in roles was extremely difficult for both of them.

This is where the "Rhapsody in Blue" becomes loud, choppy, and quite angry. As a piano player I have always been uncomfortable when one hand crosses over into the territory of the other. It never feels right, like the world is upside down. That is exactly what I picture when the mother is crossing over into the child's territory, and the child is crossing over into the parent's. When they suddenly cross back and forth with no warning, it gets even more volatile.

So how do they each get to where they belong? This takes lots of time and patience. The child resents the mother for suddenly taking over and deciding to be the parent. How dare she! He is afraid to give up that power because he has been disappointed in the past and doesn't trust her. Maybe he tries to give it a shot—and then it is too scary, so he takes it back. That is when the music gets deafening and the whole orchestra joins in.

We have a wonderful pen-pal program for our children. People from all over the country sign up to write to them. The kids love getting surprise letters in the mail, and no doubt the writers on the other end are greatly blessed in the process.

I was reading a letter one of our young boys wrote recently. He must have been asked what sports he liked, because the first line read, "I really don't like sports. After all, what do they do to solve problems in the world?"

It hit me that this boy had experienced too many grown-up things in his short little life to find any meaning in something like sports. He had recently been reprimanded in Sunday school for being disruptive, but I could see how sitting around singing Jesus songs probably seemed pointless to him. My word, his father had just gone to prison.

Is there any good news in this behind-the-scenes melody that plays day and night around here? After all, we do not have just one song playing—we have multiple songs playing at the same time. Well, yes, there is hope. And there is good news.

Let's take the little girl who left. That looks like a pretty hopeless story—but she was able to stop the madness for the months they were here and enjoy just being a kid, perhaps for the very first time in her life. She danced with other children in a dance contest, she played with the goats and chickens, and she got a glimpse of what her home can look like one day when she is a mother herself. Through counseling, she had the chance to express her feelings as never before. She saw the differences in her own mother when she applied herself, and even told us, "My mother is nicer to me here." She will not forget those memories of safety and security. She knows, now, what that looks like.

Through the years several people have pulled me aside and confessed that it is hard for them to care about a mother who does not treat her child right. But this is one thing I think they need to consider: that mother is simply a grown-up version of that innocent child. The difference is that her own mother may not have had a place like Blue Monarch to teach her how to break that cycle.

We see amazing things happen as that "Rhapsody in Blue" becomes more peaceful and the right and left hands learn to stay where they belong. But let me tell you the most valuable thing the mother and child learn while they are here.

Even though they both may have longed for a parent to care for them, they discover they actually had one all along—their heavenly Father. It is when each of them realizes this—and I mean truly believes and feels it in their heart—that they begin to heal as a family and settle into their proper roles as mother and child. We get to *see* the music when that happens...and it is a beautiful, beautiful sight.

> *Thank you, Lord, for being such a good, good Father, even when we don't realize you're there. Thank you for your powerful healing that brings such beautiful music. Amen.*

I invite you to listen to Leonard Bernstein play "Rhapsody in Blue," by George Gershwin.[1] It is such a great illustration of the intense and powerful process as our mothers and children find their places in that delicate relationship.

Update: I'm happy to report, the little girl I mentioned above stopped bringing me a list of things to discuss after school each day. Instead, she began riding bikes, climbing trees, and playing in the yard, just like a little girl should. And the boy who saw no value in sports—he made the soccer team. Thank you, Lord!

---

1 | Qiyu Liu, "George Gershwin—Rhapsody in Blue—Leonard Bernstein, New York Philharmonic (1976)," YouTube, December 4, 2014. https://youtu.be/cH2PH0auTUU.

"WHAT IN THE WORLD WERE YOU DOING DOWN THERE?"

Do you ever get so angry it makes you cry? We are fighting a powerful, destructive gang, and it is so big, the members of the gang do not even know each other or travel in the same circles. Nevertheless, they belong to a deadly group that is responsible for death, heartache, and sadness that is destroying families everywhere. We have been personally touched by this devastation, have felt its pain firsthand, and it makes me furious.

Let me introduce you to the members of this gang. They include pharmaceutical companies, medical professionals, and drug dealers. Together they have created the perfect storm, a deadly combination of greed, apathy, and pain.

When we first got started at Blue Monarch, meth was the drug of choice, by far. About the third year, however, painkillers rose to the top, and they have stayed there ever since. Through the years I have occasionally had a woman curl up on the floor of my office and literally cry because she craved painkillers so much. Never have I seen this kind of behavior because of any other drug.

We have served hundreds of women since we opened. Thankfully, we never lost even one due to drug overdose until our fourteenth year. And despite the fact that our program had become stronger and more successful, we lost two former residents within only seven short months.

There are some significant things these two women had in common. They both had plans for the future. They both left behind hurting children who will miss them the rest of their lives. And they both died from drugs laced with fentanyl, a synthetic opioid. Something else they had in common? Both their lives mattered—a lot.

So why is there such a rash of people dying from this dreadful drug? According to the Centers for Disease Control and Prevention, fentanyl overdose deaths rose 350 percent between 2019 and 2021, making fentanyl overdoses the leading cause of death in this country for people between the ages of eighteen and forty-five.[2] This is outrageous.

I feel like I have been walking around for months, desperately trying to understand this national epidemic. From a businessperson's perspective, it makes no sense to kill off your customers. So why would a drug dealer sell something that could potentially hurt his sales? I have spent a lot of time talking with our residents, whom I consider to be the experts on this topic, and this is what I have learned.

Fentanyl is cheap. So it is an easy way to deceitfully bulk up another drug to create a higher profit margin. Truth is, compared with heroin, it takes only a few grains the size of salt to cause someone to die from an overdose of fentanyl. So why are the dealers not being more careful? Simple fact: they do not care enough to be careful. And it is all about the money.

Isn't it interesting that a deadly drug like this is dirt cheap, but something like an EpiPen for an allergic reaction is outrageously expensive? Something is terribly out of balance here. There are all kinds of stories of how some pharmaceutical companies are making harmful decisions based on profits alone, fully aware they are hurting families in the process. But again, is it about the money?

Then why are opioids so prevalent and available? You do not have to research very long to see that many medical professionals (certainly not all, of course) are eager to overprescribe painkillers. Therefore, these drugs are in medicine cabinets, purses, and pockets everywhere. Perhaps the pharmaceutical industry has provided some kind of incentive for doctors to prescribe them. That is one theory. Or maybe doling out painkillers is just easier than taking the time to explore other options.

2 | "Fentanyl Overdose Deaths Are Taking the Lives of Children in Kansas City and Nationally," *Up to Date*, KCUR, October 6, 2022. https://www.kcur.org/podcast/up-to-date/2022-10-06/fentanyl-overdose-deaths-are-taking-the-lives-of-children-in-kansas-city-and-nationally.

We have had women show up at Blue Monarch with over thirty legal prescriptions. How does this happen? We get so frustrated because our residents ask doctors not to prescribe narcotics for them since they struggle with addiction, and yet they leave with a prescription for narcotics anyway. We have one woman who was prescribed medications by a doctor for seven years before she saw him face to face. One of our mothers became addicted to opioids following a surgery, and even though her doctor insisted her painkillers would not harm her unborn child, he was tragically born addicted to painkillers too.

Truth is, I think relapse has often been considered a natural part of the recovery process. We have occasionally had women leave our program and then contact us later to report that they'd relapsed. However, they are also proud to describe how they used the tools they gained at Blue Monarch to pick themselves back up this time instead of spiraling out of control. This used to be a fairly predictable pattern with a happy ending.

Let's face it—the days of the complimentary relapse are over. What is out there now is so much more potent, so much more deadly; the same amount that used to feel good will now kill you. Relapse is no longer an option.

The challenging journey of recovery often takes me back to a time when I was a child, struggling with my own challenge. I hated the water, and in fact, after a week of swimming lessons, the instructors gave my parents their money back. The last day was humiliating for my mom and dad, I'm sure, because while all the other kids were diving off the board and swimming under water to the other side, all I could do was dip my head in the water without holding my nose, and barely dog-paddle to keep myself from drowning.

Nevertheless, every time we went to the Olympic-size pool at a nearby state park, I was determined to jump off the high diving board. I really do not know why I put myself through this self-inflicted torture, but I felt some kind of overwhelming obligation to conquer my fears and overcome the challenge.

Many times I got to the top of the ladder and then chickened out. Even though the ladder was completely packed with people, I carefully backed down the ladder past every angry, grumbling swimmer until I landed safely back on the ground. "Excuse me, excuse me . . ."

This is so much like the struggle I see our women experience here. They desperately want to conquer their addiction. They want it so badly! So they fearfully climb the ladder—and even stagger back down a few times before they eventually make it to the edge of the high diving board.

The day I finally got the nerve to jump off the high board, I held my nose, shut my eyes, and then leapt into thin air. It seemed like I fell forever, and since my eyes were shut, landing in the water came as a sudden shock. I quickly struggled to rise to the surface for air and was horrified to find that someone had put a lid on the pool! I couldn't get out! I struck the lid over and over with my fist and went into a complete panic. I knew for sure I would drown.

Then it occurred to me to open my eyes. When I did, I discovered the world was upside down. What I thought was the surface of the water was really the floor of the pool. In fact, there were my father's feet in front of me.

He reached down, grabbed my hand, and pulled me out of the water. "What in the world were you doing down there?"

Sometimes I believe this is exactly what happens with people who relapse. They conquer their fear of sobriety (because there really is a fear of success and the unknown), painfully climb that enormous ladder of recovery, finally make it to the edge of the diving board, then jump off into their new lives of hope and uncertainty. But when their world gets turned upside down because of sadness, regret, discouragement, or simply feeling overwhelmed, they close their eyes and head downward for help and not up.

The deadly gang we battle is so large and out of control, I am not sure what we do to reel that monster back. What we can do, however, is follow the advice of the amazing women we serve.

When I asked the women at Blue Monarch, each one of them said the only solution was having a personal relationship with God and relying on him for strength. They saw no other way to avoid relapse and overcome addiction.

So these women who have recovered prove there is something we can do. We can tell the ones we love, who are struggling with possible relapse, "Please open your eyes, look up, and grab the hand of your heavenly Father, who is reaching for you." He does care. And this is the crazy part—it's totally free.

Thank you, Lord, for Blue Monarch—a place where women can learn the true solution to addiction and relapse. Please protect every single woman who has ever crossed our threshold, that she will look to you for help before her child experiences the pain of losing her. Amen.

"DON'T THEY KNOW ABOUT BIRTH CONTROL?"

"Why do they have so many babies? Don't they know about birth control?"

I am occasionally asked these awkward questions, so I recently put together a survey to settle this once and for all. I polled the women we had living with us at the time. Nothing was surprising. It was a collection of obvious responses:

- "I was so young I didn't know anything about birth control."
- "I was raped."
- "I was using drugs and didn't think about it."

And a very common one:

- "I wanted someone to love me."

The mothers we serve are often judged because of the poor choices they've made that have affected their children. And of course, there's always the inevitable observation about all the good people out there who desperately want children but cannot conceive, and yet this mother who has made all sorts of mistakes is allowed to have baby after baby. Yes, it is the elephant in the room. And it is a big one.

But this is the comment that occasionally rears its ugly head, feels like a punch in the stomach, and brings out the Mama Bear in me: "They should not be allowed to have any more children. They should be sterilized."

WHAT?! Ouch.

The problem is, it is impossible for me to have an unbiased opinion about this issue because I know, personally, hundreds of precious children who would not be with us today if that were a solution. They have names. They run into my office and say some of the funniest things I have ever heard. They smile, they laugh, and they cling to their mothers as if they are all that matters in the world. Their lives have value. And, quite frankly, it is not up to us to decide who can have children and who cannot.

Besides, at what point would one cross over into forbidden motherhood? Who would make that decision? And what about the fathers—would they also be sterilized?

Truth is, I have known plenty of mothers who were just as destructive to their children, but because they were not drug addicts and their dysfunction or abuse was behind a much nicer door, no one questioned whether they should be allowed to have more.

At the end of the day, it is difficult to understand some of these questions, and only God can answer them for us.

What I do know, however, is that the broken families can be healed. I have seen it happen many times.

We have seen that it is possible for a mother to become more nurturing to her children. The mess really can be cleaned up, and the family can be made whole. There is a name for it. It is called redemption—and it is a beautiful gift from our heavenly Father.

So who wants to tell this dear little girl she should not have been born because her mother made some mistakes? Seriously.

Aria enjoying life!

Lord, thank you for the beautiful sanctity of life that you reveal to us every single day. Thank you for showing us over and over that through you, we can forever change the life of a child by changing the life of a mother. Amen.

"SEAT BELT IS FASTENED. BRING IT ON!"

One of the most common questions we get is "What is a typical day at Blue Monarch?" This always makes me laugh, because there really is no such thing as a typical day. Honestly, it's like I crawl out of bed, after saying a prayer, of course, and from that point on I just hope I remembered to fasten my seat belt.

I often regret that our supporters do not get to experience what we see daily. So I decided to take you along with me for just one day. Don't forget to fasten your seat belt, though, because you may get what I call "Blue Monarch whiplash." You never know if you're going to see the greatest miracle you've ever seen, or if you're going to get your heart broken into a million pieces. And both could happen on the same day.

First of all, as I pull into the gravel driveway at Blue Monarch, I am immediately greeted by a nasty dead armadillo. Smack-dab in the middle of the driveway. I can see from the tire tracks in the grass that no one knows what to do about it. Sam, our wonderful dog, is looking a little guilty, so I suppose he is responsible for this. Nice. A quick problem to solve on my way in . . .

"Can someone please move the bikes away from the door? And there's a goat crying. Would someone please go check on it?"

As soon as I get the lamps turned on in my office, I get a call from a very special Blue Monarch friend. He offers to purchase a car for Marie so she can get to work. Marie is currently in our WINGS program for graduates, and for many weeks we have been getting her to and from work through a complicated science project made up of staff members and dedicated volunteers. Yay! Marie will have a car now. She is going to be so excited.

The car must be picked up today, so I think we should run and get the car after Kate, my right-hand development genius, and I meet a donor for lunch. In fact, we should drive it to the place where Marie works and surprise her with it. Yes, let's do it. What fun.

Kate and I have lunch scheduled with an enthusiastic, faithful donor and friend, so we gather some things she needs us to bring. The sweet woman is on a mission to introduce some of her friends to Blue Monarch, so we want to send her well equipped with lots of information. I love this woman's passion for Blue Monarch, and I'm looking forward to seeing her. She had a birthday recently, so everyone signs a card for us to take. I catch up on some emails and discuss some resident issues with the program staff before heading out the door.

While Kate and I enjoy rich conversation with this benefactor, who is one of the most fascinating women I have ever met, I glance down at my phone and notice I have a lengthy text from one of our graduates. It appears frantic, so I excuse myself and go to the restroom to read it. She is completely distraught because a fourteen-year-old boy has been sexually abusing her seven-year-old daughter. No! The mother goes on to tell me the young man has been charged with rape of a child, but the judge has basically given him a slap on the wrist. This is outrageous.

The mother is in a rage, as I can only imagine. My mind immediately goes back to the day this little girl was born. I held her in my arms in her most innocent, purest moment, totally unaware that seven years later her innocence would be stolen from her in such a vile way.

I text the mother back to let her know we will do whatever we can to help her. A little stunned, I continue to quietly process this terrible news as I return to the table and eat my barbeque as if nothing's happened. My heart is broken, and I am incredibly angry. I need to make some calls as soon as possible.

After we say our goodbyes, Kate and I leave to pick up Marie's new car and take it to the nice inn where she works. We explain to the receptionist why we need to see Marie, and she immediately becomes teary eyed. She says, "I pray for Blue Monarch every day." The supervisor fetches Marie for us, and

SEAT BELT IS FASTENED. BRING IT ON!"

as I lead her to the car, Marie's coworkers follow her. Before I know it, we have a parking lot full of people crying and hugging Marie.

Marie says, "I can't believe this! Just yesterday my supervisor said she had a message for me from God, that if I needed something, I should ask for it. So I prayed last night that God would somehow provide a car for me!" She laughed through the tears. "But that's not all. I told God I really wanted a Honda because they get such good mileage!" And of course, the car just happens to be a Honda Accord.

It is so sweet to see Marie's coworkers lift her up and share in her excitement. She is in good hands here. Thank you, Lord.

I am eager to see Xeven's reaction, Marie's son. Their relationship has improved so much in their time at Blue Monarch, it's hard to believe they're the same family. When Xeven sees the car, he immediately begins making fist pumps in the air. "Yes! Yes!" You can tell he is so proud of his mama. Man, I'm glad I didn't miss seeing that.

Then I learn that the Department of Children's Services has miraculously decided to allow Ashley to get her two boys back *today*. Wow! We didn't expect it to happen that quickly, so we scramble to get bunk beds moved into her room right away.

Time seems to crawl by. The boys are delayed because, sadly, a child in DCS custody has run away from home, and they must find him before bringing Ashley's sons. We say a quick prayer for that child.

While we wait, I check on the distraught mom of the seven-year-old girl to see if the court has provided for her daughter to receive counseling. There are many unanswered questions and hard-to-understand answers. Part of this mother's agony is because she also experienced the same thing at a young age, so, like an onion, there are many painful layers to this trauma. My heart hurts for all of them. I am angry, sad, and even a little sick to my stomach over it. Please, Lord, heal this little girl.

Meanwhile, Ashley waits, and waits, and waits at the window for her boys to arrive. How many times have I seen this sight—a mother waiting at this same window for the first glimpse of her children after a long and painful separation? I realize whenever I have seen this, there have always been other mothers surrounding her who understand the pain, the fear, and the agonizing anticipation.

Mothers patiently waiting together

Ashley has not seen her boys in eighteen months, so I am certain she has fears they will not remember her or even like her. I should tell her that in all my years of this, not once have I seen a child who did not immediately cling to his mother, even when there were years of separation. That always seems like such a miracle to me. The bond between mother and child is undeniably supernatural.

Finally! Here comes the car, and Ashley rushes out the door. The other moms want to run out there with her, but I encourage them to give her some space. So instead, they crowd at the railing and watch from the porch with tears in their eyes.

Immediately, both boys jump out of the car and hug their mom. I can see that Ashley is trying very hard not to cry in front of them, but tears of joy still cover her face.

I have seen this amazing scene over and over. In fact, hundreds of children have been reunited with their mothers through our program. But never have I grown tired of this powerful moment. It still reaches in and grabs my heart like it did the very first time.

Okay, it's 6:30 and I should go home now. Thank you, Lord, for another "typical day at Blue Monarch." I wouldn't have missed it for the world—and I can't wait to see what you have up your sleeve for tomorrow. Bring it on!

> *Do not be anxious about anything, but in every situation, by prayer and petition, with thanksgiving, present your requests to God.* (Philippians 4:6)

"STOP! DON'T SHOOT!"

It was around midnight, and I was sound asleep when all of a sudden my husband yelled, "Susan! Someone's coming down the driveway!" What?!

Clay and I live in the woods with virtually no neighbors. Unless the moon is bright, it is darker than dark with no lights in sight. Our gravel driveway is almost a mile long, and during the twenty-plus years we have lived there, I think I have seen only two wandering cars venture all the way to the house before turning around.

The vehicle slowed way down, then the headlights turned off while the car was still creeping toward the house. Once it stopped rolling, even in the darkness we could see a shadowy figure get out—and then another. As they began approaching the front porch, Clay grabbed a shotgun, and I ran for the phone. It had to be a home invasion. There had been lots of stories about them on the news lately, but they were always in the city—not way out in areas like ours. And they all ended poorly. My heart was racing as I prepared to punch in the numbers for 911.

Clay and I waited in the darkness at the door as the two figures stepped onto the porch. When they finally reached the door, Clay suddenly flipped on the porch light, and I was shocked at what I saw. Our intruders were two former Blue Monarch graduates, for crying out loud. When they saw Clay's shotgun, they both began screaming, "Stop! Don't shoot! It's us!"

My word. My first thought was *Why in the world can't you take care of anything during normal business hours?* Turned out, Amy had violated her probation, there was a warrant out for her arrest, and she had been on the run for about ten months. The other graduate was along for moral support, but needed some calming down of her own. She was a nervous wreck. Their explanation for creeping up with the headlights off was that they didn't want to wake us if we were asleep. Geez . . .

Amy wanted me to take her to jail so she could turn herself in. Again, why did this have to happen in the middle of the night, and why did she need me to do it?

Amy eventually confessed that she had come to me because she wanted someone to pray for her before she went back to jail. All right, I could do that and was honored to. We prayed together, and then Clay and I drove Amy to jail almost an hour away to be booked. By the time we got back home, it was time to get up.

I spent the next few days struggling to determine what we had really accomplished with Amy. Watching her go back to jail felt like such a failure.

Several days after this overnight ordeal, I checked the mail and was happy to find a note from Amy. Turned out it was a thank-you note, written in pencil—thanking me for taking her to jail, and thanking Clay for not shooting her. I told myself, *Well, at least that girl learned how to write a thank-you note. At least there's that.*

Thank-you notes are important to us at Blue Monarch. When someone gives us a gift, they receive a note from our residents. I hear more about these thank-you notes than anything else we do. People love them. I remember visiting a monthly donor at his office one day, and much to my surprise, every single thank-you note he had ever received was mounted on a bulletin board on the wall. He cherished every one.

It's funny how our thank-you notes are blessings in both directions. Our donors are blessed by what the notes say, and our residents are really touched that so many people out there, people they don't even know, want to give their resources to help them. Some women even get tearful when they grasp this idea for the first time.

This thank-you note process takes some training though. Not only is it the very first time most of our residents have ever written a thank-you note, but for some, an attitude of gratitude is also a new concept. I remember one first-time thank-you note in particular that needed some work. It went something like this:

*Dear [So-and-so], I think you have such a great name! I love
weird, unusual names. Do you like your name? I have always
wished my name was G.I. Jane. Don't you like that name?
Love, G.I. Jane.*

And then there was the woman who enjoyed using words she did not
know, and often misused the ones she did know. Sometimes she would even
make up a word, use it with great confidence, and just hope no one noticed.
She wrote a donor one time thanking him for "giving her an opportunity to
expose herself." Not exactly what she really meant—and definitely not something we would promote.

Sometimes I think our residents' thank-you notes are great
indicators of how far they have
grown emotionally and even spiritually. Just look at this recent note
from "G.I. Jane." She is hardly the
same person she was when she
walked in the door almost a year
ago. And now she's proud to use
her real name.

I need to level with you. I wasn't
sure I would even be able to write
a blog post today, because I have
been a bundle of mixed emotions.
We had to discharge a woman this

*G.I. Jane's improved version
of a thank-you note*

morning, and it was heartbreaking, disappointing, frustrating, and even a
little infuriating. I'll be honest. I've done a little pouting today. This woman
is so much better than some of the choices she makes. One of her children
was born while she lived here, so it was especially hurtful to see him leave.
Blue Monarch is all that child knows. And we adore her older child too, so
we will miss them both a lot. I found myself wondering what we had really

accomplished with this woman, much like I had questioned myself about Amy. This was simply not the way I wanted things to turn out. However, God has been speaking to me in a gentle way, and he has given me a good reminder that I needed in this moment.

While digging through some old files to find the thank-you note from Amy—you know, the one thanking me for taking her to jail, and thanking my husband for not shooting her—I also found a huge stack of letters Amy wrote to me while she was still incarcerated. As I pored through the pile of letters, I began to realize that each one mentioned something valuable Amy or her children had gotten from Blue Monarch during their time with us. Apparently, there were many seeds planted along the way—even though I may never know how they grow and bloom.

What was I thinking? Amy learned much more than just how to write a thank-you note. She and her children gained a lot while they were here. A whole lot.

And then it hit me. I know this is also true for the woman who left this morning. There were many seeds planted for her, and also for each of her two sweet little children.

Therefore, instead of feeling sorry for myself that we don't get to watch those seeds bloom for this family, I should be thanking God for the privilege and honor of planting them.

As I sit here and ponder this thought, I can hear God gently speaking to my heart. "You see, a seed can't grow if it isn't first planted . . . And sometimes that's all I need you to do. Trust me. I will take it from here."

Dear Lord, thank you for allowing us to plant the seeds that you continue to grow, and for the blessings that bloom even when we aren't watching. Thank you for this beautiful and amazing gift. Amen.

"SIGN LANGUAGE IS ALL I CAN HEAR RIGHT NOW."

"What's happened to you since I saw you last? You've been grinding your teeth!" The dental hygienist went on to say the damage I had done to my teeth would ordinarily take ten to twenty years to happen on its own.

Great. Just one more reason to be mad at "It."

"It" was something that had turned our world upside down. Like a thick, dark, evil liquid, "It" had permeated every single aspect of what we do at Blue Monarch. Not one thing had gone untouched.

"It" reared its ugly head on March 13 of 2019. As I was leaving a board meeting that evening, I called Jeannie before I drove out of the parking lot. I had a strange feeling that something with her wasn't quite right. In fact, for a couple of weeks, every time I had looked at Jeannie, I'd seen a vision of her fading off into the distance. It was strange, and I didn't know what it could mean. It gave me an uneasy feeling, so I never mentioned it to her.

"Did everything go okay today while I was at the board meeting?"

Jeannie is our amazing program director. You met her in the foreword to this book. Jeannie came to our program with her three little girls in 2003 as one of our very first families. I described earlier how she left after only six months, which ultimately led to four years in prison. Yet, years later she became a key figure in our Blue Monarch leadership. She is woven through the very fabric of what we do.

"Yeah, everything was good."

I was still confused by the feeling I had, so I asked about her girls, and she caught me up on how each daughter was doing. I hung up, still carrying a dark feeling in my heart that I could not explain.

Just a few hours after this conversation, shortly before 10:00 p.m., my phone rang, and it's a moment I will never forget. Jeannie screamed hysterically, "Carmen's been shot! Please pray!" Her daughter Carmen had turned eighteen just a few weeks before. Right away, an image of Carmen as a rowdy toddler flashed through my mind.

Jeannie with Carmen and her sisters as I remember them

I immediately threw on some clothes and grabbed my purse on the way out the door. "Please, Lord, no! Please don't let this happen! Please!" Right away it felt like an evil attack.

Shortly before I walked into the hospital, I learned that Carmen had not survived. I think in that moment my heart went hard. I was angry. Angry with the person who did this. Angry with the people who do things like this all the time. And most of all, angry with God for letting this happen to the sweetest person I know.

When I found Jeannie, she was a puddle of grief, suffering from every parent's greatest fear. We cried like babies, and I think it was in that moment that I became spiritually deaf. I had no interest in anything God had to say from that point on, because I was so angry with him. Why hadn't he stopped that bullet before it struck Carmen's beautiful face? After all, we know he could have.

It was shocking, really. Jeannie had brought many people to know Christ. She had touched so many lives in powerful ways—not only through her job at Blue Monarch, but through her volunteer work in prison ministry too. She had served God well, so why hadn't he protected her? I found myself trying to come up with some divine reason for what had happened—but the truth was, it just sucked. I decided right then and there that "Why did this happen to Carmen?" would be the first thing I asked when I entered the gates of heaven—right before "Where did you come from?" which had been, until then, my first question.

As I sat in the church at Carmen's funeral a few days later, I listened to all the crying and suffering from across the sanctuary. It struck me how one person's actions could cause so much pain for so many people.

This tragic event had a profound effect on our entire program. The residents we serve could make no sense of what had happened. If this could happen to Jeannie, then none of us were safe! They were also angry with God, and it manifested itself in ugly ways. They resented those of us trying to fill the gap in Jeannie's absence. They no longer trusted us. How could they? After all, they no longer trusted God either. As a group they became belligerent, bitter, uncooperative, and even disrespectful. The world felt completely out of sync.

Nevertheless, our staff members carried heavy hearts into everything they did to keep the ball rolling until Jeannie could come back. We struggled to have patience with our residents while we dealt with our own grief at the same time. We tried to do our jobs and raise money with enthusiasm—but it's hard to do with a broken heart. Yep, "It" had touched every single aspect of our organization. The ripple effect was endless.

For weeks I kept my ears shut and refused to hear anything God had to say. It was like that annoying, outdated phrase "Talk to the hand." Don't talk to me. My anger only got more intense as I walked alongside Jeannie over the following weeks—meeting with the detectives, reading the dreadful 911 report, seeing the photo of Carmen's face after she had been shot between the eyes, attending the bond hearing for the one charged with Carmen's death, all while watching Jeannie's heart just crumble day after day.

It was as if the only place that brought comfort was to go back to the moment before "It" happened. Many times, I wanted to take Jeannie's pain for a day so she could just get some relief. Too bad we couldn't sign up for shifts, the way people sign up to bring food. "I'll take Tuesday if you can take Wednesday."

But what I saw over the next few months was nothing less than a miracle.

Jeannie's relationship with Jesus has only gotten stronger through this terrible tragedy, even though she still has lots of questions of her own. Her personal story has become even more powerful as she describes "leaning in on Jesus and pulling from the heavenly bank we have as God's children." I don't know how she has done it, but Jeannie has shared her testimony with many large crowds, and no doubt, many lives have been forever changed. She has met with our residents one on one and has tenderly listened as they shared their doubts and fears with her. She has wept with them as they shared her pain.

I have watched her come to work determined to serve, even on her heaviest days. Jeannie has proven to our residents that one can experience even the worst pain without turning to drugs as a way to cope. She has taught them to cling to Jesus instead. They will forever remember her example of faith and strength, long after they leave Blue Monarch. They may even share her story with their children one day. In other words, I have seen Jeannie bring her brightest light to Blue Monarch—even in her darkest hour.

As we have gradually gotten back on our feet, I have come to realize, the ripple effect of "It" is not endless after all. Once it touched the people it was going to hurt, it was finished. And hopefully, if justice is done, there will be no more. So its power is very limited.

But the impact of Jeannie's story and Carmen's life will truly be endless. Jeannie has touched more people in beautiful ways than "It" did in harmful ways. In the same way that one sunflower can produce up to two thousand seeds, I believe with every life Jeannie touches, she will be planting many more seeds along the way, which really *is* endless.

Something just hit me. Even while I was stomping around clenching my teeth and refusing to listen for God, I see now that he was speaking to me the whole time. You see, he was saying some pretty powerful things to me through my friend Jeannie. Guess God knew that sign language was the only thing I could hear for a while, so I'm glad my eyes were open, even if my ears were not. Who knew that his voice would be such a beautiful thing to see?

Dear Lord, I guess we've got some catching up to do. Let's start with these teeth . . .

Jeannie and Carmen were very close.

Update: Jeannie and her girls were initially reunited at Blue Monarch in 2003 after she had spent some time in jail. Since that time, through our program and the tremendous grace of God, hundreds of children have been able to reestablish relationships with their mothers who had lost custody. We are proud to name this rich aspect of our program the Carmen Simmons Reunification Program, which will honor a part of our ministry that is dear to Jeannie's heart. And in this way, Jeannie and Carmen will partner together in helping others for many years to come.

Unfortunately, due to the young age of the guy who shot Carmen, he was sentenced to only a few months in jail, which was the maximum. It felt hideously unfair, since Jeannie spent years longer in prison over drug-related charges. However, he had pretty strong restrictions on his probation and was found with guns shortly after his release, which indicates he has chosen a pattern of criminal behavior for which he is being held accountable.

"DONATIONS FROM COINS ON FLOOR AT WALMART"

A group of students from a prestigious business school visited us recently. Naturally, they were particularly interested in our Out of the Blue Granola and how it works with the overall mission of our nonprofit. We have an on-site business making delicious all-natural granola where the women are offered job training and an opportunity to earn money while in our program. They are involved in every aspect of the business, and for many, it is their first job earning an honest income. Each bag of granola includes a photo of one of the women with her special story of recovery, so it is also a powerful fundraising tool.

Kayla enjoying her granola job

Before they left, one of the students asked me, "So do you think there will come a day when the granola business totally funds Blue Monarch?"

My gut reaction to that question was immediate: "Well, I certainly hope not!" What?

This answer surprised everyone, including me. My word, our granola business is something I have poured blood, sweat, and tears into for many years—doing store demos, delivering granola from the trunk of my car to loading docks behind large grocery stores (squeezed between enormous tractor-trailer trucks), and rolling boxes into coffee shops on a hand dolly. I have always wanted the business to do well because that means more jobs for more women. So why would I say such a thing?

Then I realized, if the granola business totally funded Blue Monarch, that would mean we were no longer dependent on our donors—and they are our family. I know it sounds crazy, but in that split second when he asked me that question, I began picturing specific faces of individuals who give money to us. I suppose the thought of losing them was painful to me in a way I did not expect.

For instance, we have a sweet man who began writing to us regularly after his wife died a couple of years ago. He typically encloses a twenty-dollar bill with a handwritten letter, which is usually several pages long.

Each time a different Blue Monarch resident writes him back, so he essentially has almost a dozen pen pals by now. He encourages them, lifts them up, and tells them they are special. The love he frequently expresses for his wife is good for our residents to hear. See, not all men are bad.

Or let's take this woman, for example. We had a particularly rough week at Blue Monarch recently, and all of us were excited for the weekend to get here. But on a Friday afternoon we got an unusual call from a woman who said she wanted our address so she could bring us some money. She did not want to mail it. Reluctant to give out our physical address to a stranger on the phone, and not really sure of her true intentions, we were hesitant to do so. However, after deciding she was genuine, we gave her directions and waited for her arrival, anxious to meet the mysterious woman on the phone.

When she arrived with her sister, we fell in love with our mystery woman right away. She was just precious. With tears in her eyes, this young woman began sharing how she had observed her mother in an abusive relationship for many years and wished her mother could have had a place like Blue Monarch. Her mother had recently died, and she wanted to honor her by giving Blue Monarch a tithe of what she had inherited. Amazing. She went on to describe how she would love to volunteer at Blue Monarch, but she worked at a factory, typically six or seven days a week, and didn't have the time. She had learned about Blue Monarch from an article in the local paper.

We had a wonderful visit, and before she and her sister left, she reached into her pocket and pulled out an enormous wad of cash, which was wrapped in rubber bands. I had never received a gift like this, and although I couldn't wait to see how much it was, I respectfully waited until she walked out the door before ripping off the rubber bands to count it.

As I built stacks of bills on the coffee table in my office, I began to get choked up. That big wad of cash added up to $7,600! It was an enormously generous gift—and represented a tremendous sacrifice on her part. Clearly this kind of money could have a significant impact on someone working seven days a week at a factory. Speechless and moved beyond words, our staff members just sat around my coffee table shaking our heads at what an unbelievable gift this was. Such an unexpected blessing!

It wasn't too long after that when we had another surprising gift. We received a $300 check from a new donor, and just look what we found in the memo line: "Donations from coins on floor at Walmart."

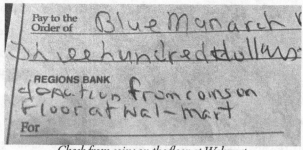

Check from coins on the floor at Walmart

Turns out, this man works in maintenance at a Walmart store. For a whole year, he collected the lost change on the floor until he saved up $300 to give to us. Can you believe that?

So, yes, I would love to sell a boatload of granola. I wish our granola was in every store across the country. But if it meant losing our Blue Monarch donors who support us so faithfully, I would have to say, "No, thank you." They mean too much. Plus, I know they are often blessed by blessing us.

Yesterday, as I was leaving to go home, I found one of our residents on the front porch crying. Her mother had been released from prison recently, and the resident was hurt that she had not heard from her. "My mother knows my address, and she hasn't even written." Barely able to get the words out, she cried, "I just want her to say, 'Hey, I'm proud of you.'"

In that moment I realized there was nothing we could do that would replace what she needed from her mother. But I was grateful she had a Blue Monarch family that would support her, lift her up, and tell her she's special. In fact, I suspect there might even be a dear old man sitting down right now, about to tell her that very thing. "I am proud of you. Keep up the good work."

That reminds me. We should send that sweet man a bag of granola. After all, he's family.

> *Lord, thank you for each and every donor who helps us become the family our women and children need, and perhaps the family they never had. Amen.*

"HOW DARE YOU GET BETTER!"

"Miss Susan! Today was a good day at school! I didn't slap, scratch, or bite anyone!"

"Well, that is certainly a good day when we don't do those things. Great job!" Everyone within earshot of this young boy cheered. "Yay!"

I looked at this four-year-old and saw how excited and proud he was to please his mother, who bragged on him as she grinned from ear to ear. The magnitude of this news might have been lost on an outsider. It really was a big deal that no one had been slapped, scratched, or bitten that day, because lately, any one of those things could happen—or maybe even all three. Again, yay!

As I leaned down to give him a hug, the boy's mother stood behind him with an expression that showed how much she loved him. This little family struggled to overcome lots and lots of trauma, most of which would cross over into the category of "horrific." I could only imagine how she might want to relish this moment as long as she could, because there was still a lot of work to be done, and it was not going to be easy.

Trauma for a young child leaves a lasting impression and can manifest itself in lots of ugly ways. Fortunately for this family, with the help of Blue Monarch, this boy and his mother received counseling and intense support to recover from their wounds. Progress is usually steady but can sometimes feel slow as molasses.

I looked at this little boy and how eager he was to make his mom proud, and I couldn't help but imagine her at his age. I was aware of the atrocities her own mother had subjected her to when she was growing up, and I realized she had probably never seen that same pride on her mother's face. Does she even know what that looks like?

In the summertime, there is something that always catches my eye and reminds me of women like this young mother. I often feel blessed to work at a beautiful farm in the country where I drive between amazing cornfields to get to my job. Every year, I spot one tall cornstalk that outgrows all the others. It towers over the other rows and stands completely alone. To me, this represents some of the courageous women we serve. They often stand alone as well.

Sadly, a lot of our residents do not get any family encouragement or recognition for their amazing accomplishments. I remember how stunned I was to witness this for the first time. A mother attended her daughter's graduation at Blue Monarch one year and was not shy about expressing her overwhelming disapproval. She fumed over her daughter's achievements and made no effort to hide her feelings as she fidgeted, huffed and puffed, and groaned throughout the ceremony. This bitter woman sat in the front row at our graduation and glared at her daughter the entire time. She did not clap, she did not smile, and she did not congratulate her daughter. As soon as the event was over, she stomped out the door. I still remember the hurt and embarrassment on the graduate's face on this one day that represented the first thing she had ever successfully completed.

Little did I know this dysfunction was something I would witness many times in the coming years. In fact, we once had a woman who resented her daughter's success so much, she tried to get her kicked out of our program by planting drug paraphernalia under her mattress, for crying out loud.

It's not uncommon to hear our residents on the phone with their mothers, desperate for a pat on the back, but receiving nasty ridicule instead. There are lots and lots of tears, and hours and hours of counseling over this very issue. For reasons like this, I am grateful our program is so individualized and long-term.

How do we understand this? How can any mother be angry when her daughter gets stronger and healthier? How can she resent her own child's recovery?

I am no expert, but I truly believe it is because it causes the family structure to crumble, and family members no longer know their roles. It's like shaking the family tree until its limbs begin to split and fall off. The family dynamics are completely thrown off kilter.

Perhaps the mother has always felt like the heroic rescuer, and when the daughter no longer needs rescuing, the mother is left confused about her purpose in the family. Or, what we often see is that the mother is also struggling, perhaps even in prison herself, and she is jealous of her daughter, who is getting better. Maybe the mother's failures become more obvious as her daughter learns what it means to be a healthy parent. And then there is also the mother who has selfish needs and simply wants her daughter to take care of her. (Like the mother who felt she was too old to be an exotic dancer any longer, so she wanted her daughter to pick up where she left off and carry on the family tradition.)

We also see siblings who resent the recovery and success of a sister. Perhaps the sibling has always been the good child, and the bad one made him look even better. But now that the bad child is doing well, where does he fit in? This often reminds me of the colorful parable of the prodigal son (Luke 15:11–32).

In this parable, a man's younger son goes off and lives a reckless, chaotic life—much like the women we serve. When he finally hits rock bottom and decides to change his life, he returns home to find a father who immediately embraces him and rejoices over his "recovery." But the older son is angry and resentful of the attention the prodigal son receives after all the poor choices he made. It's just not fair.

Of course, in this parable the father represents our heavenly Father, who will always be there. But what if the prodigal son returned home to an empty house? What if there was no one there to receive him and lift him up, not a parent, not a sibling—no one? It makes me think of a race held one year to benefit Blue Monarch. The organizers of the event did not think about a plan to celebrate the winner, so the first poor guy ran breathless through the finish line with not one person watching or cheering—well, except for me, but he didn't seem particularly moved by my enthusiasm, which was all he got. I have always wondered how such an uneventful finish made him feel after working so hard and doing his very best.

That is what often happens to our remarkable women. They work, they persevere, they cry, they struggle, they fight the temptation to give up. They do this day after day after day, until one brilliant day, they see that things have changed. Their children are listening to them for the first time. They aren't shouting at each other anymore. They aren't having "using dreams," and they no longer crave their drug of choice. They have a sense of peace and literally feel the presence of God throughout the day. They are excited about their futures for the first time. They are healing. Isn't it only natural to want a family member to share in their excitement?

Kenzie receiving a charm

At Blue Monarch we try to celebrate our residents' successes as much as possible. From time to time, we have even been accused of spoiling them. But you know what? We do it anyway. We present them with charms when they accomplish something notable. We invite them to share their incredible stories of recovery with others. We highlight their amazing journeys in the bags of granola we sell. And we try to always remember that "Great job!" goes a very long way. Remarkably, it is at Blue Monarch that some women hear those words for the very first time.

We realize this will never replace what some of our residents so desperately want from their mothers. But we do our best to make sure the children we serve get the real thing from their moms, in real time—even if it's for simply going through the day without slapping, scratching, or biting anyone. After all, that deserves a "Great job!" for sure! And the truth is, it's always easier to say it when we are accustomed to hearing it.

Thank you, Lord, for granting us the amazing privilege and honor of delivering an important message to the women we serve. Let us never forget to say "Great job!" especially when they need to hear it the most. Amen.

"BUT, WHAT IF?"

It was 6:45 a.m. on a Saturday morning and my phone chirped. *Someone at Blue Monarch must be going to the emergency room* went through my head as I grabbed the phone to see the text.

"Hey, this is Tyra." Tyra is a teenage girl whose mother was a part of our program about four years prior. Tyra wrote a touching book for school one time about her mother's journey at Blue Monarch, and all these years later it still lives on my coffee table. I typically hear from Tyra about once or twice a year. She has always been special to me.

I texted back, "Good to hear from you, Tyra! Is everything okay?"

"No, I'm in really bad shape."

"What's wrong? Can I call you?"

"I'm crying too hard to talk. I need help really bad."

"Are you thinking about hurting yourself?"

"Yes."

"Do you have a plan to hurt yourself?"

"Yes."

"Is anyone with you?"

"No."

At that point I set down my coffee cup, threw on some clothes, and took off out the door as I called our psychologist friend, Dr. Nancy, for advice, and our program director, Jeannie, to meet me on the way. The rest of the day involved a stressful two-hour drive to find Tyra, a dramatic arrival at her door with a police officer, and hours and hours of sitting at the hospital. However, the day ended late that night with Tyra getting the support she knew she needed. I was proud of her for reaching out, and I was thankful she felt Blue Monarch was a safe place to seek help.

This incident weighed heavily on my heart for weeks afterward, and there were a lot of "what-ifs" that ran through my head. What if I had not seen the text? What if I had waited too long before responding? I could hardly bear the thought of worst-case scenarios.

Seems like "what if" has been a constant theme throughout my Blue Monarch experience. At any given time, we have hundreds of families on our waiting list. We have developed a very effective, unique program with a strong emphasis on children and parenting. For this reason, we are in high demand, so it feels like we are turning people away every single day. Each time we hang up the phone after talking to a desperate and often tearful applicant, I am certain we all ask ourselves what is going to happen to her after we hang up. This is why we have been so committed to finding a way to help more families. Our entire staff feels the tremendous urgency. Sadly, there have been a few times when the applicant has died by the time we have called back with an opening.

A couple of weeks ago, we entered a whole new, very exciting chapter in our Blue Monarch history. Since 2003, I have been looking at a wire fence just fifty-two feet from my office, hoping and praying that one day we would find a way to purchase that beautiful farm adjacent to us. I was always fearful it would eventually be filled with houses, and we would lose the healing sanctuary the open farmland provided.

Each year I would ask the owner what he wanted for the fifty-eight-acre farm with the house and outbuildings, just in case some miracle happened and we could somehow buy it. There was one very scary year when the farm was officially on the market, with a sign and everything. I am not proud of

it, but when I saw potential buyers walking the property line, I would suddenly come up with an outdoor game for the women and children. The object of the game was to be as loud and obnoxious as possible— and in the process make us look like

The gorgeous view from our campus

really undesirable neighbors. As I said, I am not proud of it, but hey, a gal's gotta do what a gal's gotta do.

So, finally in 2019, some miracle did happen, and we were able to buy the farm. A very generous couple offered an amazing gift of $200,000 as a matching challenge, and in one night we were able to raise the matching funds to purchase the farm. It truly was a miracle.

The closing was held at Blue Monarch so all our staff and residents could participate. It was meaningful to me, because it was such a dramatic difference from the closing on our original fifty acres. That time I was alone in a room with a couple of realtors and a closing agent, about to sign a note for nearly a million dollars, and still in shock that it was happening at all.

This time, however, I was surrounded by the amazing women we serve, as well as our staff, who so beautifully lift me up and love our families so deeply. Unexpectedly, as soon as the papers were signed, the women began singing a beautiful song praising God for this remarkable moment. It was very moving to see how excited our residents were over the purchase of this property. As we prepared to raise the money we needed, the women prayed together on their own, asking God to bless Blue Monarch and future families in this tremendous way.

We are excited beyond words that this campus expansion is allowing us to greatly improve the services we provide, offer even richer opportunities to our women and children, and most importantly, serve more families who are hurting. We plan to build an additional eight-family home on this new property, and we are also working on the plans for a beautiful multipurpose building. After that is completed, we hope to build a granola kitchen with better truck access and an on-site daycare for our kids.

I remember, on the day I put together a detailed plan for each proposed additional structure on our new land, the square footage for each space, and the estimated cost of construction, I began to feel and absorb the enormous scope of what was about to happen. I'll be honest. Not only was I imagining the incredible blessings our women and children would receive as we doubled our population, but I could not resist picturing a double dose of frustrations as well.

Such as, the other morning when I got to work, I got out of my car and stepped onto a Popsicle stick with the nasty, gooey wrapper still attached. Great. Someone wasn't watching her child and should have picked this up. I carefully peeled it off my shoe and carried it with me as I walked across the parking lot. Great again. A bike was blocking the sidewalk, and I had to step over it. How many times have we talked about where the bikes belong? And what's this? A runaway stroller (empty, thank goodness) was blocking the steps. Who left that there? For a moment I imagined myself going through this same morning with not one but *two* Popsicle wrappers stuck to my shoes as I fought off *two* bikes and *two* strollers.

As I fantasized about the impact of doubling all our struggles, someone texted me a photograph of a mother and child that immediately put everything into perspective.

Jenn had applied to Blue Monarch a long time ago but realized the waiting list was lengthy and she might need to make other plans. She was already struggling as the single mother of a toddler, she was pregnant, trying to overcome a life of addiction, and she felt extremely hopeless. In her overwhelming desperation, Jenn scheduled an abortion in Atlanta.

However, before this day came, this day that would end the life of Jenn's baby, she received a call that Blue Monarch could take her. She saw this as a bright sign of hope and came to Blue Monarch and canceled her abortion. Cody was born last week, and the photograph on my phone captured the proud expression on that mama's face.

So are we looking at an expansion that will double the number of women and children we can serve? You bet we are. Will that also double the work, the heartaches, the challenges, and the frustrations? You bet it will.

But this is the beautiful side of that story: just imagine . . .

What if, instead of one canceled abortion, there are *two* healthy miracle babies like Jenn's baby, Cody?

What if, instead of one Tyra, there are *two* teenagers who know they can reach out to us if they are on the brink of suicide?

Now imagine this...

What if we missed out on twice as many blessings and miracles because we did not have the faith and courage to take that next big step? I don't know about you,

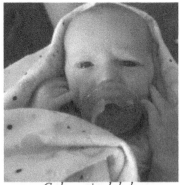

Cody, a miracle baby

but I'm glad I don't have to ask myself that question anytime soon—even if it means a dadgum Popsicle wrapper on each foot. Bring it on!

> *Lord, above all, may we always seek your will and not ours. Please guide us as we enter this exciting new chapter at Blue Monarch. You already know the names of every woman and child that will need us in the years to come. Give us wisdom and strength as we prepare to serve them well. Amen.*

part three

"Love, not judge. No, really."

The other week a couple I had never seen before sat right in front of me at church just as the service began. With multiple services, it is always hard to know if someone is visiting or just attending at a different time.

When the singing began, a woman who typically sits a few seats from me began her usual songbird vibrato tenor, which is often heard above the praise and worship team. She has a beautiful voice, which probably made her quite a catch for some church choir in the past, but in our contemporary service, I'll admit, it can sometimes feel a little awkward.

What I observed that day, though, hurt my heart. Every single time this sweet woman's beautiful voice rose above the congregation, the new couple in front of me looked at each other and smiled. Their smiles were not kind. Instead, they were exchanging very critical, make-fun-of-someone-and-laugh-about-it-later smiles.

Each time they did this, I glanced over, just hoping the woman was not aware the two were making fun of her. Whether she noticed them or not, she was simply worshiping God with her hands raised, praising him with her melodious voice, clenching her eyes in fervent prayer. There were emotional tears in the corners of her eyes.

I felt certain she was praying for great healing. Just moments before, this woman had shared with me that she was waiting for some pretty serious test results and could possibly have cancer. And yet, there she was, singing with abandon, praising God with complete trust and adoration.

I couldn't help but wonder how the insensitive couple in front of me might feel if they knew more about this woman. If they knew how sweet she was, that she would be sure to remember their names if she met them, how many immense health trials she had faced in her lifetime, the circumstances that caused her to attend church by herself—would they have behaved any differently?

This incident reminded me of a recent conversation about a life lesson I had with our residents. They had collectively decided they were not happy with a staffing management decision we had made, and I knew their rush to judgment was based on very few facts, which is always dangerous. They were acting very self-righteous and judgmental, and it was spiraling out of control. So I used a jar of beans to illustrate the process they had used to come to their group conclusion. It went something like this.

"Hey, guys, let me share a little story with you.

"Years ago, I was excited to take the women of Blue Monarch to my hometown of Franklin. It meant a lot to me to revisit the downtown where I spent so much of my time growing up, and to share it with the amazing women of Blue Monarch.

"I was so excited I could hardly wait. The downtown is nothing like it was when I was growing up. Franklin was often considered an unsophisticated hick town back then. In fact, there was a time when I played on the high school tennis team, and on one occasion, when we played a private school in Nashville, the other team yelled ugly remarks to us, like 'Who loaned you shoes today?'

"I remember looking down at my white seersucker tennis dress with blue trim and my bloomers with rows of frills, all of which I had made myself . . . and suddenly noticing that the opposing team had expensive matching outfits. When I looked around me, I realized each girl on my team was dressed in her own tennis garb, unique to her. We were all wearing white, but no two outfits were alike. And as for our shoes, they were a collection of everything from sneakers to oxford saddle loafers, and even sandals. We left our school that day feeling really special, ready to take on our opponents, but we returned feeling wounded and humiliated."

The women seemed a little puzzled as to where I was going with my story. I continued.

"By the time I took the Blue Monarch women on this trip, Franklin was no longer a hick town but had become a hip destination full of cute, unique shops, and we were going to have fun exploring each and every one of them.

"There were perhaps seven women with me, and we strolled down Main Street together, checking out the beautiful window displays and entering the little shops and boutiques one by one. I knew we wouldn't be buying anything, but I thought it would be great fun just to look.

"Pretty soon, though, I noticed there were fewer and fewer of my companions going into the shops with me. Instead, the women began waiting on the sidewalk out front. I asked them, 'What are you doing out here? Don't you want to come in?'

"What they told me broke my heart. It wasn't easy getting it out of them, but the group finally explained that they felt uncomfortable about the way people were looking at them and acting toward them.

"'What? Nonsense,' I said. 'Come with me and I'll show you, you're imagining things.'

"The group didn't want to, but they followed me into the next little boutique, and it didn't take long to see what they were talking about. One of our women pulled a beautiful blue sweater off a rack to show me, and the saleslady quickly came over and removed it from her hand with some clumsy excuse about having misplaced it. I looked around at the other shoppers. Two were clutching their purses to their chests, and one lady even looked a little scared.

"I stood back and took a good look at the women I had brought with me, trying to understand what others were seeing that would cause them to react in this way.

"As I studied the hurt and shameful expressions on the faces of the women I had brought with me, I realized the people we had seen that day were basing their opinions entirely on what little they knew and saw, which was only a fraction of what was really there. It was understandable, we've all done it, but these women who were so dear to me had been hurt, which hurt me too.

"For instance, there was Teresa, missing her front teeth. Well, they didn't know she had suffered a severe blow to the head by a steel-toed boot. She was lucky to be alive and still struggled with slight brain damage because of it.

"There was Stella, with crudely drawn tattoos all over her arms and neck. The other people in those shops didn't know the tattoos told the story of the painful death of her child, whom she was still grieving.

"And there was Melissa, with a prematurely aged face and rough exterior. There was no way for anyone to know that she grew up in a house that had no heat other than the hot air that came from the dryer vent in sixty-minute intervals. She never once got a Christmas gift as a child.

"As I glanced over the rest of the group, I was reminded that each of them had been sexually abused as a child, by someone she should have been able to trust. There was no way for a stranger to know that.

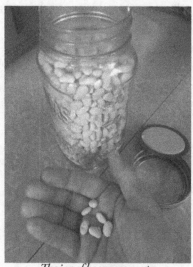

The jar of beans we use to teach this lesson

"Each person is like this jar of beans. It is full of things we don't know—circumstances, life experiences, events, disappointments, hurts, losses. But just like the people we encountered in the shops that day, we often draw conclusions from just a few beans, only the ones we can see in that moment. Perhaps our judgment would be different if our opinions were not based on such a tiny portion of the information."

And then I asked the group, "When you are the recipient of that, it doesn't feel very fair, does it?"

At Blue Monarch we live by a phrase that God powerfully gave me during a spiritual mountaintop experience a few years back: "Serve, not fix. Love, not judge." It has become our favorite saying, and in fact, I realize I am wearing a sweatshirt bearing those words as I write this.

We often focus on "Serve, not fix." But sometimes I think we overlook the equally powerful "Love, not judge."

Those we serve at Blue Monarch are easy targets for quick judgment, based on only a few facts. I am grateful for all the amazing folks who love so sweetly and support so generously—without judgment—the incredible women and children we serve.

Truth is, even though I will never know the hurt or struggle each bean represents, and it is sometimes tempting to judge from only a few, I do know our residents are the most remarkable women one could ever have the pleasure of knowing. And I somehow get the tremendous honor to serve and love them each and every day. May I always make the most of this unique and priceless opportunity.

> *Only you know what's in that jar, Lord, so help us to see others through your eyes. Give us the hearts to love before we are tempted to judge. And help us to never forget that you first did the same for us. Amen.*

"WAIT. I'VE BEEN ON THIS TRAIN BEFORE."

It had to be the greatest speaking gig ever. It was in the Bahamas. The family of a prestigious foundation invited me to speak at their annual members-and-trustees meeting after hearing my story of how Blue Monarch got started. Naturally, I accepted the invitation. Who wouldn't?

Just a few days before the trip, I received all the impressive printed material that went along with the event. It was clearly a much bigger deal than I realized. When I began reading the bios of the other speakers, my heart started to beat right out of my chest.

There was my brief little "Rebecca of Sunnybrook Farm" bio, right in the middle of a collection that represented famous scientists and dignitaries we only see on television or hear about in the news. *Oh. My. Gosh.*

I began reading more about those who would attend. The list included all sorts of brainiacs and even Nobel Prize winners. "These are Albert Einstein–type people. Or is it Alfred? Okay, that just proves my point! I don't belong!"

I immediately picked up the phone to call the family and gracefully decline. Actually, I wanted to give them an opportunity to uninvite me, because clearly there had been a terrible mistake. "No, we always hear from thinkers. We would love to hear from a doer."

So off I went to the Bahamas to get in front of a massive crowd of folks who were a thousand times smarter than I was. My stomach stayed in knots until I finally got my opportunity to speak, which was not until the last evening of the event. I stepped onto the podium and said, "Well, I have to confess, when I saw the list of outstanding people attending this meeting, I realized I had very little time to write a best-selling novel, cure a disease, or achieve

world peace—so I apologize, because I wasn't able to do any of those things."
At that point it became surprisingly easy.

I went on to tell the story of Blue Monarch, how we got started from an actual dream I had one night when I was minding my own business, and how it all eventually came true, down to the tiniest detail. I shared some of the amazing stories of lives changed and lives saved. The entire banquet hall of dignitaries respectfully listened to every word, appeared to be engaged, and responded with excellent questions.

The next morning a husky man approached me while I was eating breakfast in the hotel dining room. He said, "I was at the meeting last night and heard your talk." He had a very thick British accent, which I have never been able to imitate properly. "Did you see Chuck Colson? He was hanging on every word you said."

I hesitated. "Chuck Colson . . . Chuck Colson . . . The name sounds familiar . . ."

"Do you not know who Chuck Colson is? Were you not born in America?!"

"Wait. Wasn't he involved in Watergate?"

The man was incensed at my ignorance and began giving me the complete rundown of how Mr. Colson had founded Prison Fellowship, which had become the country's largest Christian nonprofit serving prisoners and their families, and he had become a leading advocate for criminal justice reform. This gentleman was especially offended that I had never heard Chuck Colson on the radio. *Should I tell him I don't know if it was Albert or Alfred Einstein? That would really get him in a wad.*

When I returned to my room, I quickly looked up Chuck Colson's photo on my computer so I could see if I remembered seeing him in the crowd.

Oh my word. I remembered him, all right.

The night before, after dinner when I was returning to my room, I helped a nice couple navigate their way to the elevator. The gentleman and I both grumbled about how the hotel forced its guests to travel through the chaotic casino to get back to their rooms. I remembered the man introducing himself, and later, when I asked him to repeat his name (because I had already forgotten it), he and his wife looked at each other and had a good chuckle about it. Well, no wonder.

Just a few days later, I returned to my office, and this is what was already sitting on my desk. I quickly ripped it open, and the first paragraph from Mr. Colson said, "As you perhaps know, I founded Prison Fellowship many years ago when I was released from prison for a Watergate-related offense." (My word, he was probably hoping by now I had figured out who he was.)

The letter also complimented me on my "stirring testimony." But this is the part I have referred to many times through the years when I found myself needing a good pat on the back.

My cherished letter from Chuck Colson

"I find it very amazing that you do as much as you do on the kind of budget you have." It goes on to say, "I could tell from listening to you that your business skills have been an obvious plus as you've realized the fulfillment of your dream." Ah . . . what a meaningful endorsement, especially since I didn't always have good business skills.

There have been many times when I have reached a point where the task ahead seems enormous and much bigger than I am. But I have realized there is something I refer to as the "perfect cocktail" to trudge ahead.

First, it takes a good reminder that God is in control, not me. Blue Monarch is his plan, not mine. Every time I remind myself of this, I find I can breathe again.

Second, it takes many, many folks who listen to God's call on their own hearts to share their resources and help fund the things we do. I take great pride in the fact that we have done as much as we have with what we have received. We always strive to be good stewards of what we have been given, and this is often a topic we emphasize in staff meetings.

And last, it takes the endorsement of others for us to grow and thrive. Many times, regardless of the size of a gift, it is the implied endorsement that means the most. For instance, just the other day, I was in the Target checkout line an hour away from Blue Monarch when a woman came up to me and said, "Aren't you the lady from Blue Monarch?" She shoved a five-dollar bill into my hand and said, "Here. Take this. I want to give this to Blue Monarch."

That endorsement from her meant as much to me as the endorsement from Chuck Colson. When people give of their time or their resources, they also tell us they believe in our mission, they trust us with their investments, and they are cheering us on in our toughest moments. That means the world to us—especially in times like the ones we are in today.

The year 2019 was one of the most remarkable years we ever had at Blue Monarch. In many ways I would compare it to the very beginning, when I started out each day with a trust fall. Back then I felt like I stepped onto a fast locomotive train every morning, never knowing where it would take me, but simply trusting God to get me there.

In that one year, we experienced unbelievable abundance through the generosity of many, many kind-hearted people.

- We received gifts to purchase two new fifteen-passenger vans and can now transport our women and children without the fear of breaking down on the side of the road, which had begun to happen frequently.
- Through the generosity of an anonymous family and others, we built four more cottages for our WINGS Transitional Community for Graduates and can now offer this successful extended opportunity to eight families.

Our eight beautiful WINGS cottages
Rendering by Hannah Goodgion with Hodgson Douglas

- Just one month after the purchase of the farm, we received an unbelievable promise for $825,000 to build an additional eight-family residential facility on our new property. I received this amazing news from Ben and Joan Rechter on a Friday afternoon when I could still see cows in the very spot where we would be able to build this magnificent home.

The Ben and Joan Rechter Home
Rendering by Josh Thompson with St. John Engineering

We do not take this abundance lightly. *"From everyone who has been given much, much will be demanded; and from the one who has been entrusted with much, much more will be asked"* (Luke 12:48).

After we purchased the farm, I wanted to be standing there when that "wall" of a wire fence finally came down. I imagined crossing that line along with all the women and children and staff of Blue Monarch as we held hands and dramatically took that momentous step together. But, despite all my best efforts and planning, the fence came down while I was at a board meeting, and I missed it.

As soon as the meeting was over, I raced back so I could see how it looked without the fence in place. It was not the ceremony I had envisioned, but it turned out even better than that.

The sun was going down as I jumped out of my car. I quickly walked out into the pasture with just enough light to avoid the cow patties that were still scattered across the grass. As I ventured onto this land that I had only observed from a distance, I felt like God was giving me a private viewing of what was up ahead. It was almost what people refer to as an out-of-body experience.

I stood on the spot where we planned to build the new home. I was eager to see what our women and children would see from their bedroom windows and from the front porch. I could almost smell the scent of new construction.

Off in the distance on the horizon was the gorgeous sunset that often feels like a gift just for us. It was exciting to imagine that some special women would be seeing that from their bedroom windows.

Then I looked across the field at where we hope to build a multipurpose building one day. I imagined all the powerful classes that will take place there, the children in play therapy to overcome hideous traumas, the counseling, the exercise and ballgames, the healing, the praying, the graduations, the big meals, the events, the music . . .

Then I looked at the spot where we hope to build a new granola kitchen to take on more business, which will provide more on-site jobs for our women. And next door, a daycare that will serve our children and the surrounding community as well. Not only that, but it will also provide special care for those mothers who risk losing their jobs because they have no one to fall back on when their children are sick.

And then I got even more excited as I looked at the existing cow barns and thought about how we plan to use them for horse therapy to allow our women and children an even richer opportunity to heal.

With a wave of energy and emotion, I was overcome with the realization that this expansion, when completed, will allow us to serve more than double the number we can currently house. With the hundreds of families on our waiting list at any given time, that means a lot.

As I lingered in that spot and took it all in, I glanced at the beautiful main house, which I had never seen from that perspective, behind the former fence. The lights were on, the house was full of life, there was a woman at the kitchen sink cleaning dishes from supper, and I could hear a mother and child laughing as they ran to their room at the other house. There was the faint sound of someone practicing the piano in the great room. A mom stepped outside to set her barn boots on the back porch and then hesitated for a moment to admire the sunset.

"Yes, Lord. This is what it is all about." I am not typically a crier, but I found myself standing there in the dark with this window into authentic life at Blue Monarch—and this window into *future* life at Blue Monarch—with tears running down my face. "I don't know what in the world I ever did to deserve this beautiful moment, Lord, but thank you for the train that got me here."

We are keenly aware that Blue Monarch is in a season of tremendous growth, and with that comes greater responsibility. Does it feel overwhelming at times? Well, of course it does. And yet it feels like I have been here before, because I find myself ready to step onto that train again, and I cannot wait to see where it takes me. This time, though, I'm taking a whole lot of wonderful people along with me. So, if you are one of those people, hang on—because it's going to be an amazing ride.

Lord, let us never forget to look to you for guidance, and to always remember, the glory belongs to you alone. Amen.

"QUITE FRANKLY, I DIDN'T THINK I WAS THAT BIG OF A DEAL."

As soon as the young man walked into my café, a whiff of the marijuana fog surrounding him took me right back to the '70s. He was wearing a worn-out T-shirt with the sleeves ripped off at the shoulders, and when he turned around, the back of his shirt displayed an upside-down American flag that had big X's marked across it with a broad-tipped black marker. I assumed he was there to place an order at the counter.

Much to my surprise, when I returned to the dining room, someone had given him a job application. *Okay, so this will be interesting. Now I owe the guy an interview.*

When the young man completed his application, I sat down to discuss it with him. He started with a question. "Do I have to give you my real social security number?" (What good is a fake one?)

I studied his answers and work history. The first thing that jumped off the page was that he had been dishonorably discharged from the army. Had to appreciate the honesty, but naturally I was curious.

"So why were you dishonorably discharged?"

"Well, when it started out, I was just pretending to be crazy. But by the time it was all said and done, I really *was* crazy." A real-life Klinger.

Somehow I just couldn't walk away. "Well, I see that you were an electrician's mate. Did you like that kind of work?"

"Oh yeah! I *loved* it!"

"So I'm curious. Why aren't you looking for an electrical job, working with an electrician?"

He leaned over the table and motioned for me to come closer as if he had

139

something private and very important to share with me. The herbal, skunky aroma was even stronger now, and I couldn't imagine what his secret might be.

Then he whispered, "It's because I don't *be-lieve* in electricity." He cocked his head and slowly nodded at me, as if he was sure that we shared the same radical idea. I couldn't help but wonder if he knew he was moving in slow motion.

"Well, I hate to tell you, we use a whole lot of it here. You would be miserable, so I don't think this will work out." He must have misinterpreted our brief encounter, because a short time later, he was picked up for public drunkenness and apparently told the officer to contact us because he was sure we would take care of him.

The other day I was thinking back on how many people I had interviewed and employed in my lifetime. I believe, including my horse farm and boarding operation, my vacation rentals, my bakery/café, Out of the Blue Granola, and Blue Monarch, it's been hundreds of people. So I feel like I have seen and heard it all. But it was because of one individual Blue Monarch woman that I developed an intensive nine-week Work Ethics course that I have been teaching our residents since 2007.

It was that same year when Brooke, a Blue Monarch resident, had become the Saturday morning baker at The Blue Chair. It was a pretty important job, because this was our biggest day of the week. On this particular morning, Brooke did not show up for work, which created an enormous crisis for us. I called to see what had happened to her. She very nonchalantly said, "I had problems with childcare . . . and quite frankly, I didn't think it was that big of a deal." Really?

"Well, it *is* a very big deal, and we will talk about it on Monday." In that moment I realized we had a huge issue concerning good work ethics, and we needed to solve it—not just for Brooke, but for every other Blue Monarch resident as well.

At that point, I basically developed our Work Ethics course from all my own bad experiences employing the population we serve. When I sat down to crunch some numbers and see what Brooke's negligence had cost The Blue Chair that morning, I began to look at other events involving the women I had employed from Blue Monarch, and I soon realized my business had suffered a five-figure loss over the past year because of their poor performance and lack of good work ethics.

Despite its unfortunate beginning, teaching Work Ethics has ended up being one of my favorite parts of my job. A resident does not take the class until she is close to graduating from our eighteen-to-twenty-four-month core program. By this time, she has other intense recovery, healing, and growth behind her, and now she can focus on her future and a job.

This rich course has proven to be very effective in developing successful, conscientious employees. In fact, nearly half of our current staff consists of Blue Monarch graduates who have taken this course. As with Brooke, we first take an honest look at past work performance and the impact it had on former employers and businesses. We assign a dollar figure to any damage, and this often results in tears when they discover how negatively they impacted the places they worked, which is important for them to understand. I remember the moment when one woman realized she was the very reason the company went out of business. She was devastated to grasp what she had done to them. This exercise includes writing a letter of apology to former employers, and some of these letters are even mailed because their writers sincerely want to make amends.

Then we walk in the shoes of the employer for a while to develop empathy and see that the boss is not always the bad guy. (Why do so many think he is? I've never understood this.) Then we begin to explore unique gifts and strengths. I love this particular class because we don't leave until we have a list of twenty strengths for each person. With every strength we identify, the smiles on their faces get bigger and bigger. We continue to explore interests and narrow down realistic possibilities that can become an exciting job or career, not just a paycheck. Finally, we prepare to do our best in order to obtain that job and keep it.

Back when I did jail interviews myself, I would always ask this question: "What are your dreams for the future?" Each answer was the same and consistently came with a blank stare. "I've never thought about it."

I finally realized, when one has focused most of her life on sheer survival, where is there a place for dreaming about a career or future? Nevertheless, I continued to ask the question anyway. I was always hopeful it would plant a seed and cause someone to begin thinking about it.

In my class, however, I get the amazing opportunity to see the light come on for the very first time: the moment when a woman begins to truly believe in her heart that she is valuable, that she is capable, and that she can realistically have the job or career that only seemed possible for others. "Wow. Maybe I really can do that . . ."

Sometimes women in my class have never envisioned anything other than drawing disability benefits, simply because that is what everyone in the family does. "Hmm . . . so I don't have to do that? Really?"

I have often wondered if my office literally lights up and hosts of angels begin singing in this powerful moment when one of our residents gets a glimpse of an exciting future for the first time. Some women cry, some struggle to hold back a grin that feels out of control, and some sit in a sort of reverent, stunned silence as they gradually process what could potentially happen. It is powerful. It is tangible. You can almost see the ground shake as they begin to see themselves in a totally new light. It is overwhelmingly gratifying and gives me chills every single time. Man, I love it!

For instance, I will never forget the moment Lauren realized she could become a pilot—and in fact she can fly a plane now, all by herself.

Or the day Courtney realized she wanted to be a medical assistant, and now she has a wonderful job at a doctor's office.

However, I believe I am the one who has learned more from this course than anyone else. All those years when I hit bumps in the road because of the things Blue Monarch women did (or didn't do) on the job, I always attributed them to being lazy or inconsiderate. Otherwise, how do you explain an attitude of "quite frankly, I didn't think it was that big of a deal"?

What I have learned, however, is this: When a woman feels she holds absolutely no value, she cannot imagine how her absence makes a difference. If I have nothing to contribute, how can it possibly matter if I am not there? After all, who would give me something important to do? What she's really saying is, "Quite frankly, I didn't think *I* was that big of a deal."

As a child, my father told me over and over, "You can do anything you put your mind to." I believed him simply because he said it. Many of the women we serve have also believed things they have been told. Such as "You are stupid, worthless, and ugly, and you'll never amount to anything." Can you imagine looking at your future and seeing nothing but a dark, blank wall?

God has given me the amazing privilege to look a woman in the eyes and tell her, "I believe in you. You can do anything you put your mind to." And if it works like it's supposed to, she will gradually believe what I have said . . . the room will begin filling up with a bright light that only I can see . . . and best of all, her children might get to hear those same words before the day is out. Yeah, I absolutely love my job.

> *Lord, please help us to show each woman we serve the bright and amazing future you have in store for her. Help us to instill a sense of hope in every child, and to teach our moms to always lift them up. Amen.*

"EVIL, YOU'RE GETTING SLOPPY."

Evil,

You must find it amusing that some people don't even think you are real. No doubt that must create a pretty fun playground for you. Those of us at Blue Monarch, however, know very well that you do, indeed, exist. We know your face, we recognize your voice, and we are familiar with your stench and the path of destruction covered with your footprints.

But from the number of tearful phone calls we are receiving, and the stacks of desperate applications in the mail, it appears you have gotten sloppy. You see, in order for your evil plans to work, you must maintain a sensitive balance with the ones you torment. The destruction of the soul must be slow and steady, so much so that the victim barely notices the decline. The light must diminish one ray at a time until there is complete and total darkness. Otherwise, your cover is blown, and people wake up.

You have a couple of weaknesses that give you problems, though, and I'm sure you know what they are. Pride and greed. It's hard for you to resist

bragging about the things you do, so you can't help but leave clues where people can find them. And nothing is ever enough, so you tend to overreach. That's when you get sloppy. That's when people open their eyes and see you for what you really are.

Do you know the signs when you

Heather reflecting on the pain

cross that line and get ahead of yourself? Well, let me describe a few of them to you . . .

The high you made so incredibly euphoric suddenly becomes nasty and disgusting. A glamorous life of crime turns into waking up at the base of a filthy toilet. The friends who were the only ones who truly understood and cared reveal that they steal from anyone and everyone with no remorse. The love letters from the perfect man somehow turn into black eyes and chipped teeth. The people in authority who were stupid and ignorant begin saying words of wisdom that oddly ring true. And here's where you really mess up. The children who meant nothing and were in the way—even the ones still safe in the womb—suddenly become valuable little people who deserve much better from their mothers.

You see, there are many over whom you still have enormous control and power. Their lives are miserably chaotic, which developed so gradually, nothing felt out of place. In fact, you created entire family trees so full of despair, one more victim simply blended in completely unnoticed. But apparently, for many others, you totally overshot and got greedy. You made their lives so extremely painful, disgusting, and wretched that they began looking for help and thankfully found us.

What you haven't figured out is that rock bottom actually works for us. That's where we see the greatest desperation and commitment for change. It's from that ugly place that the most powerful transformation takes place. Your insatiable desire to push deeper and deeper just gets them there quicker—so you are essentially helping us. Wow . . . that must hurt.

I should probably warn you: we are fighters, and we don't give up easily. We never intend to give them back to you. In fact, as the amazing women we serve begin to experience the joy and hope of total freedom from the despicable life you offer, you will become nothing more than a dim and distasteful memory. There truly is a point of no return. We know this because we've seen courageous women reach that place many, many times, and the evidence is undeniable.

So, until the next time you get sloppy, we will be waiting. You'll slip up. It's just a matter of when. And we will be ready.

Sincerely,

Blue Monarch Warrior

> *The thief does not come except to steal, and to kill, and to destroy. I have come that they may have life, and that they may have it more abundantly.* (John 10:10 NKJV)

"PLEASE DON'T LOVE US TO DEATH."

This may sound terrible, but back when I was the one to interview potential residents in jail, I loved to find a woman who had reached rock bottom. I looked for the telltale sign she was really there: she had lost everyone.

She would often be a woman who collapsed onto the metal table where we talked, crying uncontrollably, not even concerned about how she might look to the other inmates or officers wandering in and out of the room. She was completely broken and would tell me, "I have no one." And I was happy to hear it.

The reason I liked to find a woman who had truly reached rock bottom was because I knew she had the greatest chance for success. She was the one who would probably make it. Why is that? Because she finally had to rely on herself to seek help—and there was no one to fall back on. It was up to her and her alone. Truth is, as long as there is someone out there who will bail her out (literally and figuratively) every time she messes up, why change? It is working.

But what does it take to get to that point? It takes everyone around her letting go. Yes, it takes letting go.

This is something that comes up quite often as we talk with parents, grandparents, friends, and advocates who want to help someone they love. They know they shouldn't give her money again. They know they should probably let her sit in jail, and they realize they are enabling her—but it is so hard to say no. I get that.

I often compare this advice to what they tell you to do if you come face to face with a shark: be still and do not move. Seriously? That just completely goes against nature and everything your body instinctively tells you to do. Saying no to your child who is asking for help feels just as unnatural.

So I had this on my mind one day and decided to ask the experts what they thought. I spent some time talking with the amazing women we had at Blue Monarch at the time to get their thoughts on the subject.

Here are some of the interesting things I learned:

First of all, I asked them if they thought it took getting to rock bottom to make the decision to come to Blue Monarch. Every single one immediately said, "Yes." Interesting.

I asked them to describe what rock bottom meant to them. Each woman said it was when she had lost all support. One said, "It took my family leaving me for good to finally make me break." Another said, "It wasn't until I lost everyone's support that I really started to look inside myself." And this: "I finally realized I was about to become another statistic and my baby was going to be a ward of the state."

I asked a tougher question. "For the parents out there who are afraid their daughters will hurt themselves when the parents finally have the courage to say no, what advice do you have? Are they really running that risk?"

"Helping them more is only fueling them to go further down—so what's the difference?" They all nodded and agreed. They also began giving examples of when they had threatened suicide or said others would hurt them, just to get what they wanted.

So I asked, "What should people do then?" All at once, the women began throwing out answers to my question—and it was clear they were quite passionate about what they had to say.

"Have faith that God will save them!"

"Don't make bond—let them sit there."

"For sure, don't give them money whatever you do."

"Pray for them."

"Don't believe all the lies."

"Don't answer the phone." (And this was coming from a woman who had been living under a bridge at her lowest point.)

"Tell them you love them—but be strong and don't give in."

Then they began offering words of encouragement beyond the pain.

"After they get better, they will see where your love was."

"They'll appreciate it later."

"They know their family will return."

"Coming back to life makes you understand why your family did what they had to do."

"They will thank you for loving them like you had to."

At that point, as if they had rehearsed it in chorus, they all said, "Please don't love us to death!"

So there you go. Tough words from women who have been to rock bottom and know what it takes to climb out.

There's one more reason I love to see a woman who has lost all support, and it is by far the most important. Sometimes I think it takes looking around and seeing no one before she is finally ready to reach for Jesus, which is the greatest help of all. That is why rock bottom is such a beautiful place. It is from there that some of the greatest healing truly begins.

So do you know someone who needs to find rock bottom? It's actually not such a bad place after all.

> *When Jesus spoke again to the people, he said, "I am the light of the world. Whoever follows me will never walk in darkness, but will have the light of life." (John 8:12)*

"ONE OF THESE THINGS JUST DOESN'T BELONG."

Seems like we have been hearing a lot lately about child trafficking. I can hardly wrap my head around this disgusting crisis. In fact, the word *child* should never end up in the same sentence with *trafficking*. As they say on *Sesame Street*, "One of these things is not like the other. One of these things just doesn't belong."

Over the past few weeks there have been reports of unaccompanied immigrant children being flown into small Tennessee airports in the middle of the night and then leaving on multiple buses . . . to go where? What in the world? Why do we not hear the rest of the story? Are we all assuming someone else is looking into it?

There were also news reports recently about 150 missing children who were found in the state of Tennessee. And similar reports surfaced in other states across the country. I had so many questions. Why did my phone not go off 150 times with an Amber alert for each child? Why did we not see 150 signs flashing over the interstate, and where are the 150 happy reunions with tearful parents?

I made some phone calls, contacted state politicians, and did a little research to see if I could get answers, and what I discovered did not make me feel any better. After everything I learned, I am even more alarmed about the children getting off those planes. Even our government officials are having trouble getting complete information, and the details just seem to be spinning. Hearing the stories and watching the videos of this same scenario across the country made me want to cry and scream at the same time. I think it is easy to forget that every single child has a name and a face and is probably confused and afraid, not to mention homesick. I suspect there are lots of tears and there will be more in the days to come.

As for the children in our own backyard, apparently many of the missing children in Tennessee simply got lost within the system; children who were placed by the state with one person and somehow ended up with another. Some were runaways. This explanation was presented as if to say, "At least it wasn't child trafficking." Well, that may not be the case. Child trafficking can take on a lot of different shapes and sizes.

Since about 2019, we at Blue Monarch have seen a dramatic increase in the number of children, even as young as three years old, who have been victims of sexual abuse.

Every single day we observe the short-term and long-term impact of this abuse on the women and children we serve, and we know the time and tremendous work it takes to heal from the trauma. On top of that, after a crazy season of quarantine, I feel we need to brace ourselves for the stories we will hear going forward. In fact, at Blue Monarch we are even taking measures to strengthen our children's program to address their trauma when these little ones show up on our doorstep.

Honestly, this whole issue has really been heavy for me. There have been a number of times through the years when I have tried very hard to report what was obviously child sexual abuse—and it went nowhere. I remember a three-year-old girl who was molested by her grandmother's boyfriend, and after months of taking all the necessary steps, the entire investigation came to an end simply because he denied it. Case closed.

Or, in the case of another, because the pedophile was considered such a fine, upstanding man, no one would listen to my suspicions. As a result, the abuse continued undetected for years, and now that it is finally out in the open, it will take even longer to address the damage.

I went to bed recently with such a grieving heart. "Lord, there are so many children hurting. I feel so helpless because I can't seem to make a difference. How can we stop these monsters?"

That same night I had an interesting dream. I was trying to get to Blue Monarch. My trip was longer and more difficult because I was traveling on foot for some reason. When I got just a mile or so from our campus, I came upon a busy intersection where I found a very long line of little, shiny red cars crossing the road in single file. Each miniature car held only one child. They reminded me of the child-sized cars I loved to drive at Fair Park in Nashville as a kid.

Suddenly the long train of mini cars came to a halt, and several of the children hopped out to stop traffic and help me cross the road. There was a young girl in particular who seemed to be a little older and directed the others as if she was in charge. I noticed right away that her freckles and strawberry blonde hair looked familiar.

The children seemed to be very happy as they giggled and chatted among themselves. As soon as they escorted me across the intersection, they cheerfully waved, got back into their little cars, and continued on their way as if they were excited to reach their destination.

The next morning, as I reflected on the curious dream, I thought back on the young girl who had looked so familiar. Who was that?

Suddenly I realized who she was.

There was a day when I felt an overwhelming need to visit a family that had lived at Blue Monarch years before. This is not something I typically do, but I could not get this nagging thought out of my head. So I got in touch with the mother, found out where they lived, and made arrangements to visit one day after school. She did not seem particularly excited about my visit but agreed to let me come by their house.

It was great to see her kids and catch up with them. They had grown quite a bit since I had seen them last, and they were so excited to see me, they talked on top of each other as they reminisced about their favorite Blue Monarch memories. I noticed many of their most cherished ones involved their mother's accomplishments. The mom casually leaned against a car and stayed to herself as I talked with her children.

At one point a man walked out of the house, got into the same car, and left. All four kids looked at each other and immediately stopped talking. Red flag.

Finally, one child looked at the oldest and said, "You need to tell Miss Susan."

"Tell me what?"

This eventually turned into a long, detailed, very ugly, and troubling story of repeated sexual abuse. The victim was the oldest sibling, who had freckles and strawberry blonde hair and was now a preteen girl.

Sick to my stomach, I drove away in a rage over what this disgusting man had done to this girl who had been so innocent and unharmed when I had seen her last. I remembered how she used to run into my office after school with grades that made her grin from ear to ear. She was so proud. I reported the abuse right away and was relieved to see that a case was opened a few hours later.

Of course, after making a report like this, I always wonder how things transpire and what kind of drama unfolds behind the scenes. I couldn't help but wonder if this girl would be angry with me, because it was obvious who had made the report. I had to do it, but I hoped she would understand that it was to protect her.

Amazingly, a few weeks later I ran into this young girl and her family in a nearby town. The mother was angry and grumbled about all the trouble I had caused, but the freckled girl immediately ran up and gave me a big bear hug. That was my answer. It sure was nice to see she still loved me. Her brother, who had urged her to tell, hugged me even harder. I couldn't help but notice the young girl looked prettier than she had the last time I had seen her, almost as if she had become a child again.

Later, as I reflected on how this had turned out, I also thought back on how happy the children were in my dream. And then in my heart, I heard God say, "There have been lots of children rescued because of Blue Monarch—and there will be many more in the days to come. Sometimes the difference one makes is not visible to anyone but me."

He called a little child to him, and placed the child among them. And he said: "Truly I tell you, unless you change and become like little children, you will never enter the kingdom of heaven.... And whoever welcomes one such child in my name welcomes me. If anyone causes one of these little ones—those who believe in me—to stumble, it would be better for them to have a large millstone hung around their neck and to be drowned in the depths of the sea." (Matthew 18:2–6)

"MISS MARY, WHAT'S THAT CRYING IN THE KITCHEN?"

This was an early Saturday morning routine that began in second grade and continued until I went off to college.

Without knocking, I would enter the front door of my piano teacher's very large, dark, historic Civil War home in downtown Franklin, Tennessee. Immediately, the ammonia smell of up to thirty-three Siamese cats would take my breath away. Past the massive, somewhat depressing tapestries on the walls and the dark, oversized furniture, I would make my way to the grand piano in the "pah-luh," take a seat, and begin playing. Cats would wrap around my legs and sometimes crawl across the keyboard, swishing their stinky tails under my nose as I waited for Miss Mary to surface.

Eventually, Miss Mary would enter the room dressed in a shirtwaist dress with a belt she frequently adjusted, thick stockings with pumps, and pearls around her neck with matching ear bobs. Her snow-white hair was evenly divided into two buns, one over each ear, both carefully contained with white hairnets. She would also have on a little too much rouge (yes, the real thing) and lipstick that wandered outside the wrinkled lines.

Miss Mary would approach the piano clinking a dainty cup and saucer of strong instant coffee, and she would usually have biscuit crumbs in the whiskers on her chin. Miss Mary had never married and lived alone the entire time I knew her—except for one crazy summer when she rented a room upstairs to a colorful girl who had a constant flow of "gentleman callers," which Miss Mary mistook as the sign of a popular young lady with lots of friends. Even as a young girl, I knew there was probably much more to that story . . .

One Saturday morning there was a strange new sound, much different from the usual meow of a Siamese cat. It sounded like a baby crying, but I could not imagine anyone asking Miss Mary to babysit. Finally I asked her, "Miss Mary, what's that crying in the kitchen?"

"It's my new cat!" she said excitedly. "He wandered into the yard, and I'm keeping him in the kitchen until he can adjust to his new home."

I really wanted to see this cat that made such a strange sound, so she agreed to let me peek through the door as long as I didn't let him escape. The other thirty-some cats were clearly upset about this new family member and were darting around the house in a sort of fearful, chaotic frenzy. I soon learned why.

Much to my horror, when I cracked open the door, there in the middle of her linoleum kitchen table stood an enormous wild bobcat! It arched its back and showed its fangs when it saw me, and I couldn't help but notice that Miss Mary had somehow put a rhinestone collar around its neck. The kitchen was completely destroyed as if a wild animal had been turned loose in there—which was exactly what had happened.

Miss Mary's complete household had been turned upside down by her attempt to help this one animal that clearly did not want help.

I slammed the door shut. "Miss Mary, that's a wild bobcat!" I had seen enough stuffed ones at the Nashville Children's Museum to know what I was talking about.

"No, no, he's just having a hard time adjusting to his new home. He'll be fine in a few days." She said this with an odd sense of confidence.

All week I wondered how Miss Mary and the wild bobcat were getting along. And for the first time, I was excited to go to my lesson.

The door was unlocked as usual, so I carefully stepped inside and walked to the piano, listening for any sign of the bobcat . . . or Miss Mary. Nothing. The only cats I saw were quietly cowering behind the furniture. Was it possible the bobcat had killed Miss Mary? For a few minutes, I have to confess, I wondered if perhaps this might mean the end of my Saturday morning lessons. I immediately felt guilty for even thinking it.

Finally, Miss Mary appeared, not from the kitchen as usual, but from her bedroom, which I had never seen. I quickly caught a glimpse of her mysterious private space and could see she had not made her bed. She looked like she had been in a terrible wreck. Her little white buns were hanging from their sockets, her pale, thin-skinned arms were covered with deep red gashes, her silk brocade dress looked like she had slept in it, and she even had a black eye.

"Miss Mary, what happened to you?"

She reported that her new cat "never did adjust to his new home," and she had had to let him go. She had loved him, cared for him, fed him, and showered him with gifts, and in the end, he did not appreciate any of it. She seemed completely bewildered. I could only assume the bobcat was probably wandering around Franklin with a rhinestone collar still fastened around its neck.

So how does this story have anything to do with Blue Monarch?

Clearly, the bobcat did not belong in Miss Mary's house in the first place, but her reaction to this bobcat is so similar to the many calls we get from folks who are desperately trying to help someone they love, someone who is struggling with addiction and poor life choices.

"Why does she keep doing this? I pay her bills, I take care of her children, I even gave her a car . . . I've done everything for her!" They love this family member so much they are willing to sacrifice whatever it takes—even if it jeopardizes the peace and safety of everyone else in the home. They allow their homes to turn into complete and total chaos, because in their minds, this sacrifice shows how much they love this person. They insist on keeping the bobcat in the kitchen, even though the needs of the rest of the family— and probably their own needs—are greatly suffering.

This is so, so hard to accept—but sometimes the best love one can show is to give that individual the freedom to fall. Even the biblical prodigal son did not figure things out until he had lost all support, been on his own, and lived with the consequences of his choices. When he wanted to leave home, his father did not go running after him or bribe him with gifts. He let him go. This son did not come to his senses until he got so low, he had to feed pigs to survive.

I realize this sounds terrible, but some people simply have to feed pigs. It is possible that the longer we protect them from doing so, the more we delay their recovery rather than help them. After all, if we can just have the courage to trust God, then let go and let them fall, it is quite possible they will eventually land safely in his arms. Sometimes reaching this level of despair is what it takes for us to finally turn to him for help.

In fact, you know the part of the story where the father runs to meet his prodigal son who has returned with a new heart? Well, we get to see that happen here. We see the courageous women we serve run to our heavenly Father with renewed spirits and open hearts—and he receives them with open arms as if they never left. And I can tell you—it is a beautiful sight that I would not trade for anything in the world.

> *I waited patiently for the Lord; he turned to me and heard my cry. He lifted me out of the slimy pit, out of the mud and mire; he set my feet on a rock and gave me a firm place to stand. He put a new song in my mouth, a hymn of praise to our God.*
> (Psalm 40:1–3)

"I WAS AIMING FOR HIS HEART!"

Some of the women we serve have good, healthy fathers who love them and want the very best for them. Sadly, that is not always the case.

We were sitting around the kitchen table eating lunch, and somehow the topic of broken noses came up. I was surrounded by six women in our program, and it came as a shock to me that I was the only one at the table who had not suffered a broken nose at the hands of an abuser. What? I had no idea this was so common. I was impressed they didn't all look like Sylvester Stallone.

One of the women began telling a very graphic story of how her boyfriend beat her up, and oddly enough, the broken nose was not the worst of the story.

As if I was talking to a girlfriend about her husband leaving the toilet seat up, I casually said, "Well, I hope you got him back."

"I got him back, all right! I shot him!" Okay, I didn't see that coming.

"Seriously? Did you kill him?"

"Well, I meant to! I was aiming for his heart, but at the last second, he bent over backwards just like Gumby, and the bullet went through his shoulder instead."

"And then what?"

"I called the po-lice and told them I shot a man and was trying to kill him. He rolled around in the street and squealed like a pig until they got there." Apparently, her boyfriend didn't press charges, said it was an accident, and even though she insisted it was not, they did not arrest her. Guess he figured the next time might be worse.

Later, as I reflected on this woman's family tree, I realized this was practically a tradition in her family. Her mother shot her abusive husband in the neck and somehow didn't kill him or serve time. And rumors are, her grandmother shot and killed her husband, shoved his body off the bluff, and burned the sofa he was sitting on. The way it was told to me, the law looked the other way because the grandfather was a monster, and everyone knew it. The women in this family set the bar pretty low for finding a good man.

One must wonder, why did three generations of women choose men they would someday want to kill? Did the men start out charming and then change after they were together? Or did the women's partners remind them of their fathers, who were just as bad? Is it true little girls grow up to marry someone just like their fathers?

I am reminded of a day when I chatted with the women at Blue Monarch about relationships and discovered not one of them had ever been on a real date—despite the fact that each one had multiple children. Sadly, not one of the mothers seemed to find this unacceptable or even unusual. In other words, they did not believe they deserved better. Changing this perspective is not easy.

Recovery is so much more than just sobriety. True recovery is a wheel with many spokes. Thankfully, Blue Monarch is a long-term program, so we have an opportunity to address the entire wheel, and our goal is to make sure there are no broken or missing spokes by the time the women walk out our door.

Choosing healthier relationships is just one of those spokes, but it is a challenging one that can seriously impact the next generation. Never was this clearer than it was last week. I received a heartbreaking call from a former resident, a call that has played over and over in my head ever since.

"I have finally hit rock bottom, Miss Susan." This woman was crying so hard she was practically hiccupping the words and it was difficult to understand her. But this part I got loud and clear: "My husband raped our little girl. Twice."

My heart sank and I thought I might throw up as she shared the gruesome details. My mind immediately went back to the tiny baby who was born into such a safe, nurturing bubble while at Blue Monarch years ago. This man had taken a perfect little flower and assaulted her in the most hideous, disgusting way possible. And now her father was gone, which was also going to be hard for a child to understand. I remembered a picture her mother had sent me years later of this innocent little blonde-headed girl wearing a pink-and-purple outfit, standing so proud and happy—totally unaware of what she would endure in the months to come.

"They're offering him twenty years."

In my opinion, twenty years was not nearly enough for what this little girl will carry for a lifetime. I reflected on all the women we had served who had experienced the same violation by their own biological fathers. It was only through the tremendous grace of God and his supernatural healing that some were able to overcome the trauma and heartbreak—and even forgive. It was no wonder they turned to drugs to numb the pain, and I prayed this little girl would not do the same.

"I just never thought my daughter would get hurt. She's my only child!"

I thought back on all the many times we had warned the mom to get away from this man. There were many red flags she'd chosen to ignore. I wanted to turn back the clock and try again in some other way that might have gotten her attention and changed the outcome. *Please, Lord, can we go back to before this happened and try again?*

This mother is a perfect example of someone walking out the door without all the spokes intact. She is a fierce survivor, extremely bright, funny, resourceful, and full of promise for a great future. But she can also be very hardheaded and stubborn. Despite the fact that she was clean and sober when she left Blue Monarch, and had accomplished some amazing things, she was not willing to let go of her perspective on relationships. In other words, she still wanted to do recovery her way and hang on to pieces of her old life at the same time. She insisted on pursuing a relationship with a man she already knew was not healthy, and she will suffer the "what-ifs" the rest of her life. Turns out that one broken spoke was a big one.

The next day, as I looked around the room at the women we have today, I didn't want to ask, "Who's next?" I wanted to shout, "NEVER AGAIN!" I wanted to do whatever we could to ensure that no one else experienced this same trauma. We talked about the importance of completely surrendering our lives to Jesus and submitting to the process, and how destructive it can be to have one foot in recovery and the other in old behavior. It simply does not work.

So many times, as we talk about our loving heavenly Father, we get blank or even angry looks from the women we serve. How does that make any sense when their earthly fathers have been harmful or abusive? No doubt, this concept will be very difficult for the little girl who was just raped by her own father.

We pray this precious child will one day understand that her heavenly Father loves her, and she will always be his perfect little flower. He is the Father who will always be there, no matter what, and he is the Father who will never change. No matter what. Our prayer is that one day, this little girl will set the bar really, really high and seek a man with a heart like God's. May she aim for *his* heart and find it.

> Lord, we pray for tremendous healing for this little girl and her family. May she feel your presence in big and powerful ways and find comfort that only you can bring. Amen.

"ARE YOU HURT?"

It was a calm, ordinary sunny day, and I was traveling down the mountain on Highway 41 on my way to work. The sky was a brilliant blue, and the view of the Pelham Valley was spectacular as always. Best I can remember, I was going about forty miles an hour, and despite the many irritating drivers who tend to straighten the curves by crossing the center line on that road, I was staying in my lane as I always do.

My view driving down the mountain to work every day

Suddenly I heard a rough, deafening noise that I could not identify. Then, in the blink of an eye, something violently landed on my car and smashed it like a bug. Honestly, it was as if a piano had fallen out of the sky, because I didn't even have time to skid to a stop. My car was stopped in its tracks in a split second. *Whoa! What just happened?!*

It took me a moment to realize it was a tree. Branches and leaves completely engulfed my car, and there was barely enough light to see that the roof had caved in and the dashboard was completely destroyed. The cheerful music on the radio felt oddly out of place with such a destructive backdrop, so I turned off the key to concentrate. I searched for my glasses and finally found them under the brake pedal. I struggled with my door, but it wouldn't open, so I managed to slide out the other side.

When I saw the damage from the outside, it was truly shocking. The tree had landed right down the center of my car, from bumper to bumper. Wow! What a mess.

My first instinct was to call Blue Monarch. "Just wanted to let you know I'll be late. A tree just landed on my car." In looking back, I don't know if that was an underreaction from shock or if it was an indication of my unpredictable Blue Monarch world, in which such an event was barely notable.

A car slowly crept around the carnage, and the driver rolled down his window and squeamishly asked, "Was the driver killed?"

"Nope. I am the driver." Surprisingly, that car and several others just drove by, and no one stopped, which in looking back seems a little odd.

I called 911 to let them know what had happened. "Are you hurt?"

"Hmmm . . ." I hadn't thought about it. I looked down, did a quick examination, and replied, "Oddly enough, I am covered in millions of tiny pieces of glass, but I don't even have a scratch." It was a miracle.

Needless to say, the car was totaled. The guy who towed it called a few days later. "Lady, I've been sitting here looking at your car, and I've decided you are either the most blessed person I know or the luckiest person I know. So I was just wondering if you would buy me a lottery ticket."

One would think, after surviving something that should have killed me, I would come away feeling pretty invincible. Just think. Even a split second earlier or later could have made all the difference between life and death. Not to mention, even the accident, exactly how it happened, really should have killed me, or at least caused severe injury.

But I did not feel lucky or blessed. Instead, I seemed to be convinced another tree would fall on me at any moment. I became keenly aware of what was over my head, and many times I caught myself leaning away from the trees when I drove up or down the mountain. It had happened once. Who's to say it won't happen again?

The reaction from others was almost as surprising as having a tree land on my car. I cannot even count the number of times people interpreted what had happened by immediately placing the blame on God. Seriously?

"God must be teaching you to slow down and smell the roses."

"God must be trying to get your attention, and you aren't listening."

"God wants to teach you a lesson of some kind. Wonder what it is . . ." Really?

It was shocking how many people immediately jumped to the conclusion that the accident was something God had done to me for some nefarious reason. And my reaction was always the same. "Are you kidding? I believe God protected me!"

But if I am honest with myself, did I really believe that? If so, why was I so concerned it would happen again? Why was I leaning away from the trees on the side of the road as if I was always in danger?

Apparently, my faith was limited. I believed God had protected me, but I did not trust him to do it again.

That's a hard thing to admit, because my entire Blue Monarch journey has been built on tremendous faith. It has required supernatural faith every single step along the way—almost like beginning each day with a trust fall. I'm a professional faith person! So if I live with that level of conviction daily and still have limited trust in God, how in the world do we expect our deeply wounded women and children to trust him or anyone else, for that matter?

We are always puzzled by how hard it is, and how long it takes, for our women and children to trust us. In many ways we are the trees on the side of the road. No wonder they lean away from us for so long. They have been hurt many times by others—so who says they won't get hurt again? And again?

It has occurred to me recently that we face a much greater challenge than even addiction or abuse. It is faith. Teaching our families that God is not the bad guy. After all, many of us are taught from an early age, "God will get you!" As if he's just sitting around like a villain, twisting his moustache between his thumb and index finger, just waiting for us to mess up so he can catch us in the act. Bam! Got another one!

There is also a common, twisted theology that God puts us through bad things just to test our limits, as if he enjoys pushing us to the precipice to see if we will break. I have heard so many times, "Why did this happen to me? I thought God would not give me more than I could handle." They are usually referring to things God did not give them anyway—such as actions of others or even their own poor choices. After all, there's that pesky thing called "free will." It must be so frustrating for God to love his children so much and still be thought of as the bad guy.

God is not the nasty one who made the tree fall on my car. He is the one who, despite all his other concerns that day, noticed the exact time I left my house, how long I lingered at the post office, how distracted I was because of a song on the radio, how far I swerved to miss a squirrel, and still made sure that when that tree fell, my car was positioned just enough this way or that to protect me from getting hurt. He was paying attention to every detail. Every single detail. *That* is the God we want our women and children to know.

The other day I looked back at the many graduates we have had at Blue Monarch since we opened our doors. It has been an honor to present every one of them with a well-deserved diploma. As I reflected on each of their names, I wanted to see if there was a common denominator among those who have found freedom and have thrived the most. And I found it.

The graduates who have surpassed even our greatest expectations are the ones who figured out this important fact: As long as they are leaning toward their heavenly Father who loves them, it really doesn't matter if a tree falls on them again. Either way, he will take care of them. And honestly, that is what you call real faith.

Once again, my greatest teachers are the ones we serve.

> *Though you have not seen him, you love him; and even though you do not see him now, you believe in him and are filled with an inexpressible and glorious joy, for you are receiving the end result of your faith, the salvation of your souls.* (1 Peter 1:8–9)

"ARE YOU STILL TEMPTED TO DRINK HAND SANITIZER?"

Her toddler was not sleeping at night, and this mom was struggling. Allison felt exhausted, overwhelmed, and defeated. Nothing unusual for a typical mom, but for one already insecure about her parenting skills and having lost custody of another child because of her personal choices, this took a normal frustration to a whole new level. She believed she was a parenting failure, and her child's insomnia only confirmed her convictions.

Our team discussed a few options to help Allison's little boy sleep, and I handed her a bottle of lavender spray I had on my desk that had been given to me as a gift. "Here. See if this will also help."

I was a little disappointed by her reaction, which was not in proportion to the sacrifice I had just made. I really liked the lavender spray and enjoyed using it in my office, but she seemed noticeably indifferent and even a little hesitant to take it.

Little did I know, this mom had been hiding an ugly secret. She was a severe alcoholic and knew she would be at risk of drinking the lavender spray, simply for the tiny bit of alcohol in the bottle. We were also unaware that she had been drinking hand sanitizer to get a buzz. Yes, hand sanitizer. We typically don't keep liquid sanitizer around for that very reason, but she had found some left over from a recent event and had also sneaked a few bottles back from trips off campus. (Apparently the burning sensation going down the throat is a close substitute for the real thing, and the numbing it provides is worth the disgusting taste.)

When these indiscretions were finally revealed, they explained a lot. For months we had been struggling with this mom to make progress, and despite all our efforts, we still felt we were working harder at her recovery than she was. Truth was, we were.

After multiple chances, Allison left us with few options. It was frustrating because we all saw her potential and we adored her little boy, but no matter how much we tried, she was determined to remain stuck right where she was. We just continued circling the same tree.

Our staff had a lengthy meeting and finally made the painful decision to make room for someone more desperate for an opportunity. After all, we had a responsibility to honor the journeys of all the women who were putting 100 percent into their own recovery. It was imperative that we held others to the same standard. But that did not mean we had to like it. We decided to meet with Allison the following morning to let her know our decision, and we all went home with heavy hearts.

The next morning, I was hurriedly walking through my bedroom about to leave for work when a scene much like a movie unexpectedly started playing in my head. In vivid color and great detail, I saw a family of three facing a casket that held the body of a blonde-headed woman. Their backs were to me and blocked the woman's face. Where did that come from? Her husband looked to be in his early forties; he was tall and thin, with neatly cut dark hair. He was comforting their teenage daughter, whose head was tucked under his arm as she wept. To the left of the girl was her brother, who seemed to be about ten years old. He stood like a soldier, very stoic, staring at his mother in the casket with his arms by his sides, hands clenched into white-knuckled fists.

The grief was overwhelming, and I could feel this family's emotions as if they were my own. Even when I tried to shift my thoughts to something else, I couldn't. The movie in my head continued to play as the father attempted to comfort his two children while he was clearly devastated by his own loss.

I was still puzzled by this scene when God spoke to my heart. "If you discharge Allison today, this mother will be killed by a drunk driver." Wow.

All the way to work I pictured this family in my mind. It was so detailed, I was convinced I would recognize them if I saw them on the streets, and I suspected they lived in a town about an hour away where Allison would be returning if she left our campus. It was tempting to find them just to validate the powerful images.

As I walked into my office, our staff members were already preparing for our dreadful meeting with Allison. I said, "Can we call a family meeting instead with all our residents and staff?"

The atmosphere was tense because Allison's peers suspected she was leaving for all the obvious reasons, but they were puzzled by the group meeting, since this was something we would typically handle in private. They were also a little weary from trying to help her in their own ways. Allison was tearful and even trembling. She knew she had pushed her limits and was dreading the bad news.

"I wanted to include everyone instead of meeting with Allison privately because I feel the entire community needs to know what has happened. As you know, we have struggled with Allison for months, and she refuses to make any progress. We keep landing right back where we started. I know you are frustrated with her too for not being more serious about her recovery when she has so much at stake." Everyone nodded.

Allison continued to cry and tremble. I was anxious to put her out of her misery.

"But Allison is not leaving today, and I want you all to know why, because she ordinarily would be, considering the circumstances." Allison nearly collapsed on the sofa and was a bundle of tears and disbelief before I could even explain the reason. She took a noticeable deep breath.

I continued by telling our residents and staff what had happened earlier that morning and that I was going to listen to God and not discharge Allison that day. I couldn't make any promises if she continued to be uncooperative, but for today, she was not leaving. There were tears everywhere I looked. No one could believe the inevitable had shifted so dramatically.

Later that day, Allison came into my office. I expected her to express how grateful she was for another chance, but she also shared a story that clearly had a profound impact on her.

With tears streaming down her face, she said, "Miss Susan, last night I prayed my heart out that God would speak to you somehow and convince you to give me another chance. So when you told your story this morning, I couldn't believe it. God heard me! I am so thankful!" She wept tears of true gratitude and disbelief.

Well, I am happy to report that this event was a game changer. Allison became a completely different person. She became genuinely happy, with a smile that never ended. She dug into her issues with our counselor instead of holding back and refusing to talk about her true feelings. She faced the shame she carried about her secret relapses and confessed all the embarrassing details to her peers. She let go of constantly comparing herself to others, which had always been such a powerful stumbling block. She was happy to do her chores rather than grumbling behind our backs, and in many ways, she became an effective leader. She also enjoyed being a mother in a way she had never known before, and her relationship with her child visibly grew.

One day I asked Allison if she was still tempted to drink hand sanitizer. She immediately said, "No, but I haven't really been around it either."

Then she paused. "Well, I guess I have been around it at the store... and the doctor's office..." A huge smile spread across her face as she realized she no longer looked for it and was no longer tempted by it. In fact, she appeared to finally be free from that terrible temptation. Just look at that!

But there's more. From what Allison told me, her toddler was sleeping much better, which came as no surprise. Looks like he finally got the mama he was trying to find all along—and we're pretty happy to have found her too.

Lord, thank you for guiding our steps even when they take us in a different direction to unexpected places. You always know the path that is best. Amen.

"CAN I PLEASE WAKE UP AS A BIRD?"

There have been times when I have gone through an emotional rough patch and have prayed that I could please wake up as a bird. Was that too much to ask? I just wanted to quietly soar in the clouds with no problems in sight. In fact, this is the first item on my list of things to do when I get to heaven one day.

I love the sky so much, I have flown in almost every contraption there is: ultralight airplane, seaplane, glider, parasail, 1940s open-cockpit airplane, and an almost-two-mile zipline at over 11,000 feet in elevation, which isn't a plane but went so fast it felt like flying. I am fascinated by clouds, and this has been my screensaver for years. This photo is from my window seat on the way to visit some nice donors in Texas one year.

My favorite photo of clouds from my seat on a plane

Several years ago, Clay and I stopped to watch some skydivers near our home because it was something I had always wanted to do. As I stood and gazed at the jumpers, a young woman asked, "Are you thinking about jumping?" Was she talking to me? I looked around because I was surprised that she could see me. I was keenly aware that I had become strangely invisible to some people her age.

"Well, to tell you the truth, I have always wanted to skydive," I told her. "So I wanted to watch for a while to see if I could do it."

And here it came. The girl leaned closer to me, as if I couldn't hear, cocked her head in a way that she probably thought was endearing, and in her best baby voice said, "Well, it's never too late . . ." I think she even patted me on the shoulder.

I looked at Clay and said, "Never too late? What did she mean by that?" And then it hit me what she meant. *Oh my word.* I was steaming, and if I had been wearing different shoes, I think I would have marched into the hangar right that moment and signed up.

Honestly, getting older has been a little clunky. I never believed it would happen to me, although I'm not sure how I thought I would avoid it. I have reluctantly had to make some rules for myself, such as no fringe (okay, well, maybe less fringe), no dancing in my car, and no more clothes from stores whose names include the words *twenty-one* or *wet*. It's been a difficult transition, because in my head, I'm still thirty-five and skinny.

As I stood there a little wounded, processing what had just happened, I listened while the young woman chatted with her boyfriend. He was concerned they might not get their turn to jump before it was too dark. That's when she pointed to the sky and said, "But it won't matter if it gets dark down here—because it's always lighter up there!"

Okay, that made her comment sting a little less. Obviously, she was an idiot.

It did cause me to ask myself, why was I not skydiving when it was such a dream of mine? I finally realized it was something Clay always said to me whenever I entertained the idea. "Susan, have you thought about what would happen to Blue Monarch if something happened to you?" Suddenly the whole idea looked very irresponsible, because honestly, I wasn't sure how to answer that question.

Well, one day I looked around me and realized this was no longer a concern. We have the most amazing, gifted team we have ever had, each staff member a rock star in her own right. Blue Monarch has never been in better hands, which makes my job more exciting than ever before. My dream could finally come true. (You know you're confident in your staff if you're willing to jump out of a plane.)

I had the enormous privilege of skydiving with Lauren, our former Blue Monarch graduate and current staff member who has recently gotten her license as a pilot. I remember walking through the kitchen right before one of my Work Ethics classes a few years ago and Lauren saying with great distress, "Miss Susan, I just don't know what I want to do with my life . . ."

Honestly, I was a little concerned that Lauren might fall back into addiction if we didn't find something to keep her excited and motivated. That's when it hit me. Just a few days

Lauren and me after jumping out of a plane

before was when I had stood on the sidelines watching the skydivers with the young lady who made the stupid comments. "Lauren, what about the field of aviation?"

She immediately latched onto that idea, which quickly led to a Blue Monarch miracle of sorts. I invited Jim, a pilot friend and donor, to meet with her to discuss all aspects of aviation. It was in that meeting that Lauren expressed her desire to become a pilot, and Jim amazingly offered to help her get her license and loan her his own plane to do it. Jim even had a friend by the name of "Grumpy," with thirty-two years in the air force under his belt and an endless list of awards, who agreed to be her instructor. It was unbelievable.

This path has been anything but easy. Lauren has stretched herself beyond limits she never knew she had, and she has jumped through a million hoops to prove to the FAA that she is no longer an addict and can handle the responsibility and pressure of flying. No doubt, many weaker individuals would have quickly folded.

It has been one of the hardest journeys I have ever witnessed, but Lauren has persevered through many tears, endless study, countless surprise drug tests, ridiculous delays, multiple medical evaluations, and lots of sleepless nights. However, every single time she has flown solo, she has praised the Lord and worshiped across the sky, giving him all the glory.

One of the greatest thrills of my life has been to see Lauren fly over the Blue Monarch campus. It makes my heart skip a beat every single time, and it's so fun to see all the women and children run outside to cheer her on. Sam, our dog, goes nuts because he thinks he owns even the airspace over our property. Every one of those women walks back into the house believing in herself a little more, and I'm convinced even the children begin to dream bigger in that moment. The impact is tangible and shows on their faces.

So I got to jump out of a plane at 14,000 feet, dropping at 120 miles per hour, with someone whose incredible journey I have watched from a front row seat, which felt very symbolic. It was truly a dream come true and an intense thrill that I have relived in my head a hundred times.

I didn't think anything could compare to that thrill, but when Lauren finally got her pilot's license after nearly a three-year struggle, I was honored to be her very first passenger. It was almost an out-of-body experience as the two of us flew over the Blue Monarch property and I was able to see the women and children run outside and wave at us . . . from Lauren's perspective this time.

Lauren's story will be a Blue Monarch legend. I see every day the impact her determination has on the women of Blue Monarch. It gives them hope and teaches them not to give up, that their hard work and perseverance will eventually pay off. They absorb it and take it to heart.

Lauren owning the sky

As I watched Lauren so confidently maneuver the plane, manage all the many instruments and gears, communicate by radio in a cryptic language only pilots understand, and gaze across the sky as if she owned it, I couldn't help but think back on the woman who had sat in my office and wept with overwhelming brokenness, and absolutely no hope, just a few years ago. My word, look at her now. She is not just a fighter. She is a warrior, inspiring other warriors just like her.

I realize now, the young woman I met at the airstrip that day was no idiot after all. It *is* never too late. And it truly is lighter up there—even if it's dark down here. Maybe it's because the magnificent sky feels just inches away from heaven. In fact, I think if we had thought about it sooner, Lauren and I could have touched the face of God while we were there. We'll have to remember to do that next time...

> *Lord, thank you for a place where women and children can*
> *dream big, believe deeply, and achieve intensely. And thank*
> *you for my front row seat, for which I am so grateful. Amen.*

Update: Lauren is on our staff as case manager when she's not soaring in the sky on her days off. She interviewed a young woman recently who applied as a potential resident. Lauren asked her, "What makes you want to come to Blue Monarch?" The response was, "I've heard that a graduate of Blue Monarch was able to become a pilot!" Lauren was able to say, "Well, that pilot is me."

"GRRRRRRRR!"

When this adorable little girl arrived at Blue Monarch with her mom and siblings, I couldn't help but think of Nell, the young woman played by Jodie Foster in a movie by the same name. Nell had developed a strange language of her own, which was a combination of her deceased mother's distorted speech following a stroke and a secret language Nell had shared with her twin who had died decades earlier. Nell lived a life of isolation and had not been exposed to anything different.

This young girl at Blue Monarch, let's call her "Sadie," would rush into a room and aggressively lunge at random individuals, scrunch up her face, and basically growl. Yes, growl. It wasn't a mean growl. It was more of an "I don't know how to express myself, so grrrrrrrrr!"

She rarely spoke, but when she did, her words were totally unrecognizable. As with Nell, Sadie's family members were the only ones who understood her unique language. It must have been so frustrating for Sadie to see people glancing at each other with puzzled expressions instead of responding to what she was saying.

Naturally, the first time I witnessed this, my instinct was to protect Sadie from kids at school who might be cruel to her. I couldn't bear the thought of other children making fun of her odd form of communication. We needed to get her into speech therapy right away!

Sadie was interesting to observe, and I often thought she would make a rich character in a good southern novel. She was fascinating. It was obvious she was drawn to others, but like a suspicious puppy, she jumped back just in time if anyone reached for her. She was good at judging just the right distance to avoid being touched. It was a mystery how she determined which ones to approach and which ones to ignore. There was really no category in between.

As part of our recovery process, the courageous women of Blue Monarch deliver their "Readiness Statements" to their peers and our staff. This is a powerful, often very emotional, and even painful account of the difficult journey they traveled that landed them in a place like Blue Monarch. We have discovered that this exercise brings great freedom. They express their desires to do something drastically different, and they identify the individuals they wish to hold them accountable. The stories can be horrific and even shocking. I have yet to hear one that is not heartbreaking. I often wonder how they cheated death despite all the close calls. It's a miracle, actually. That's the only explanation I can come up with.

But these stories are also when I fall in love with their children and begin to see them in a whole new light. When we hear the experiences their little ones endured—and survived—we suddenly understand their behavior. The screaming immediately becomes less annoying, the crying becomes more meaningful, and their constant need for attention is totally understandable. It's as if a veil is lifted, and the child transforms into a tiny person who desperately needs our help instead of a loud, unruly kid who is out of control.

When I heard Sadie's mother describe her personal journey, I completely understood why this woman cried nonstop for the first two weeks at Blue Monarch, and why her beautiful daughter only growled at others. It suddenly made all kinds of sense. I could see why Sadie either never learned to talk or refused to talk by choice. No wonder. In fact, I found myself cheering her on. "You go, girl! You talk when you are good and ready!"

Sadie did begin working with a speech therapist, and in the meantime, she and her family settled into their new lives at Blue Monarch. She loved our pets and farm animals. She developed friendships with the other children at Blue Monarch. We focused on Sadie's recovery as much as we did on her mom's, and the little girl thrived with everything our robust children's program had to offer. Sadie was a happy child and knew she was in a good place. Her brother even pulled me aside one afternoon to tell me, "Miss Susan, you know what I love most about Blue Monarch? I know we are safe!" Sadie seemed to know that as well.

It took almost a year, but one day I suddenly realized Sadie had broken through many of the barriers she'd faced when she had first arrived. Sadie had just gotten home from school when she ran into my office with a million questions. "What's this? What's this?" She was a little old for that type of question, but I was happy to answer every single one. She jumped into my lap, gave me a hug, looked out the window at the house we were building for more families, and said, "Look! That's our new house!"

I realized in that moment that I understood her speech completely, and it was not because she and I had become family. It was because Sadie was becoming a new creation—just like her mom. If you ask me, that calls for a victory cry—like a big fat "Grrrrrrr!"

Now that I think about it . . . perhaps that's what it was all along.

"YEAH, BUT THAT'S A MIRACLE."

The restaurant was one of my favorites and the dinner was amazing, but the conversation made it difficult to enjoy. The guests around the table quickly established their positions on the evening's topic, and there was no question where everyone stood.

The purpose of the gathering was to engage in robust, and hopefully productive, dialogue with several doctors regarding the use and effectiveness of medical-assisted treatment for addiction, which had gained increasing popularity across the country. We had been invited by our board chair, Dr. Myers, who had found himself in the middle of what had become a pretty sensitive argument among recovery communities. With me were several of our staff members who had found freedom from addiction, no longer struggled with cravings for their drugs of choice, and felt no need to white-knuckle their recovery the rest of their lives. Dr. Myers felt that our perspective and experience were important to share.

The tension in the room quickly escalated as both teams expressed deep passion for their personal convictions. Even the servers seemed a little uncomfortable as they tried to quietly slink in and out of the private dining room for fear of getting caught in the crossfire. The doctors, as much of the medical community agreed, felt medical-assisted treatment was necessary to achieve sobriety. We, on the other hand, felt it was simply exchanging one drug for another and that an individual was still not sober if taking it. Many of our residents had used this method before coming to Blue Monarch, and we had not heard one success story. In fact, quite the opposite. Most of them had abused the substitute drugs or become even more addicted to them than their original drugs of choice.

With lots of enthusiasm, we offered numerous examples of women who had been able to find complete freedom from addiction without the help of a substitute drug, and each time Dr. Parker, sitting next to me, quickly responded, "Yeah, but that's a miracle. Yeah, but that's a miracle. We're trying to plug the dam before it breaks!"

We were getting nowhere. The group couldn't even agree on the definition of *sobriety*. When I realized this, I giggled at the futility of it all, and Dr. Parker immediately turned to me and said, "Do you think this is funny?" He seemed disgusted.

I looked at him and felt his frustration. He was a doctor in a neonatal intensive care unit, and I could only imagine the trauma and sadness he had seen, probably daily. No wonder he had passionate feelings about recovery. I had seen, firsthand, the terrible effects on babies who were born addicted, and it was not a pretty sight. Heartbreaking was a better description.

It occurred to me that we were focusing on miracles when Dr. Parker was in crisis mode saving lives. It made me sad, really, because I found myself wanting him to consider a miracle as one of the tools in our tool belts, but I could see that the Blue Monarch version of a miracle was not something that could be administered in an instant to the hundreds of thousands of people who were dying from overdoses. He had a point.

I felt certain Dr. Parker believed in miracles and probably saw them on a regular basis in his line of work, but I found myself feeling that our supernatural examples were somehow being discounted in our discussion. I wanted to stomp my feet and say, "But miracles still count!" Just a simple "Wow!" from someone around the table would have made me feel better.

Since Dr. Parker delivered babies, I felt compelled to tell him one of my favorite miracle stories—the one about Trenton, the Christmas Miracle Baby—but the atmosphere didn't lend itself to that type of story, so I quickly dismissed the idea.

As I drove away that evening, I realized both camps would never meet in the middle because we had entirely different missions. They were looking for a heartbeat, and we were looking for a healed heart. Yet we needed both.

After all, we sure couldn't heal a heart that was not beating. The best solution would be if we could all somehow work together.

Months later we had a fundraising banquet at Blue Monarch. It was a spectacular night under a circus-size tent with hundreds of folks who had been invited by carefully selected table hosts to learn about our ministry. As I looked out across the massive sea of people, I was shocked to find the face of Dr. Parker, the one who'd sat next to me at the awkward dinner months before. I was excited to see him, because on this night, even though I did not usually do so, I planned to tell the miraculous story of Trenton's birth. Oh, good. Dr. Parker would get to hear my favorite miracle story after all. What a coincidence.

As I stood before the crowd and shared that unbelievable experience, I described how the doctor had come into Chrystal's room and said, "I'm sorry, we have tried everything and are not going to be able to save your baby. If you want to see him alive, you only have a few minutes left."

Although I did not say this out loud, I briefly recalled the doctor's delivery of such terrible news, and I remembered thinking how this young doctor had probably already been impacted by the sadness and trauma he witnessed in his line of work. As I continued my story, I glanced at Dr. Parker seated in the crowd, and he looked visibly uncomfortable, which did not surprise me. He probably thought I was heading back down that miracle rabbit hole, and here he was a captive audience.

I described how the doctor had said that the baby's blood oxygen level had to be over 90 and it had already dropped to 20. Then my favorite part of the story: I shared how I sat there holding that tiny little hand and watched the number drop as low as 11 before I realized I needed to pray. That's when I recruited my daughter and her friends to pray for him too. And then, as I prayed while listening to Christmas carols in the background, even with my little faith, I watched the blood oxygen level steadily rise until it reached over 90 again!

But this night at the banquet was quite different from any other time I had shared that experience.

I went on to say, "Whenever I tell this story, someone always asks, 'How is Trenton doing today?' Well, you know what? Let's just ask him."

I motioned to my table and said, "Trenton, stand up and tell us how you are doing."

Trenton standing with the crowd cheering

It was a breathtaking moment, because Trenton, as a healthy, robust fifteen-year-old young man, shyly stood up and waved to everyone. The crowd went nuts. It was a powerful moment that still gives me chills. Tears were flowing. (As I often say, "If you ain't cryin', we ain't tryin'.")

Immediately after the event ended, before I even got out of my chair, Dr. Parker ran over and crouched down in front of me, which was surprising for so many reasons. The look on his face was an expression of complete awe and wonder—almost with the innocence and excitement of an eight-year-old boy. I didn't know what to expect.

"You are not going to believe this. I think I *am* that doctor."

Oh my word. I looked at his face and suddenly recalled a younger version of him walking into Chrystal's hospital room fifteen years earlier. Yes! "Oh my gosh, I think you're right. I recognize you now!"

"I was working at that same hospital when Trenton was born. And that sounds like something I would say."

"Yeah, it does, doesn't it?" We both laughed.

Well, what do you know... a doctor I so desperately wanted to embrace miracles found himself in the middle of one that had as many facets as a perfectly cut diamond. Apparently, I wasn't the only one who wanted him to hear this story, because just look at all the intricate pieces that had to fall into place for this moment to come together. I can only imagine the profound impact that revelation had on this man's heart.

So I would have to say Trenton's birth is a miracle that counts, all right. In fact, it has counted more than once. And to think it all started at the beginning of this Blue Monarch journey with a simple prayer and faith smaller than a mustard seed.

Just imagine what can happen if we start out with more.

> *Truly I tell you, if you have faith as small as a mustard seed, you can say to this mountain, "Move from here to there," and it will move. Nothing will be impossible for you.* (Matthew 17:20)

"WE'RE GLAD YOU FINALLY SHOWED UP."

What do John Glenn, Elizabeth Taylor, and Batman have in common? When I was a kid, I wanted to be all three of them. John Glenn was my hero, so naturally I wanted to be an astronaut one day, until that dream was shattered by my obvious challenges in math. (Many years later I had the great privilege of meeting John Glenn at his home, and that remains one of my greatest thrills. I will never forget all his magazine covers hanging in dime-store frames down the hallway as if they were ordinary family photos.)

Then there was Elizabeth Taylor. As I've said, for whatever reason, as a child I was absolutely fascinated with her multiple husbands—and I confess, I chipped away at that goal through the years until I decided to stop at three. That's plenty.

But it was Batman who probably influenced me the most when I finally got my driver's permit, the minute I turned fifteen years old. A few days later, while my parents were away from the house, I decided to try out the car. My family lived in a quiet subdivision on a dead-end street, which looked like a perfect spot to practice some of the Batmobile maneuvers I had seen on TV.

I grabbed my little brother, Doug, and put him in the car with me. Not sure if I wanted an accomplice, or if I was stretching the "extra driver" requirement, but he was going with me. I pulled the harmless-looking baby-blue Volkswagen hatchback onto the street and decided to see how fast I could go between our driveway and the turnaround at the end of the street.

I stomped on the gas pedal, we peeled down the street, and when we reached the end, I slammed on the brake pedal, yanked the steering wheel to the left, and let the car spin until we did a complete 360. It was awesome.

Naturally, I wanted to do it again and again. Doug tried to bail at one point, but I grabbed him by the collar and jerked him back inside the car. By golly, we were in this together. (His version is a little more dramatic.)

After a few trips up and down the street, spinning around and spewing gravel everywhere, it was on one of those trips back that I accidentally overshot the driveway. The car violently bounced off the culvert and landed in the yard. Needless to say, we left behind skid marks and tire tracks that were impossible to repair before my parents got home—so it was not a secret for long.

April 15, 2003, marks Blue Monarch's birthday, and I remember that first day like it was yesterday. The closing on our beautiful property was a month before, but on April 15, a day most people dread, I was finally able to get the key and open the door for the first time.

I will never forget that moment. I turned the key in the lock and walked into the main house. The previous owners had sold it completely furnished because they were moving out of the country, so it already looked amazing. Everything was spotless—but it was supernaturally quiet. Not a sound.

As I walked into the kitchen, I suddenly got an overwhelming, panicky feeling of "Oh my word, what have I done?!" The magnitude of this enormous undertaking hit me like a load of bricks. I even got a little dizzy from the endless "what-ifs" going through my head.

Our main house on campus
Photo credit: Britt Simmons

Then immediately God reminded me, "This is *my* plan, not yours." He showed me what the empty kitchen would look like one day when it was filled with women and children and lots of laughter and completely full of life. Whew! That was a relief. It was way too scary to think of this as my plan.

I glanced over to the sofa where I had met with the owners for the first time. I remembered telling them how God had meticulously described Blue

Monarch to me in a dream years before, and how I wanted to use the home for women and children to heal together and start a new life. And I couldn't help but reflect on the powerful moment when the owner of the property looked at me with tears in her eyes and said, "We always knew God had asked us to build this place for someone else to use one day—and we always thought it would be for women who were hurting. We're just glad you finally showed up."

But what an amazing ride it has been. I have seen lots of babies born who most likely would have died if their mothers had not come to Blue Monarch. I have seen women find complete freedom from hideous traumas and harmful addictions. I have seen hundreds of children reunited with their mothers when they were inches away from never seeing each other again. The miracles have been so remarkable I sometimes feel like each day brings more blessings than any one person should expect in a lifetime.

As we approach Blue Monarch's twentieth birthday, I have also given a lot of thought to things I wish I had done better, things I wish I had done sooner, and things I hope I never do again. I realize, as an organization in its final teenage years, we still have a lot to learn.

This is the funny thing though. As I have recalled the absolute lowest points, and the times of adversity that brought me to my knees, they all lead to the same place. Every single time, I placed myself in the driver's seat and tried to solve problems in my own power when I had only been given a learner's permit. I never was given the authority to drive on my own. I should have trusted God more and I could have made things easier on myself and those around me. I should not have underestimated his power and abundant blessings, because his plans are always grander than my own. There should have been more prayers of "Lord, please show me how to drive" instead of "Lord, why did I just run off the road?"

God has been so good to us. He has provided abundant blessings. One of the special blessings I never overlook, though, is the daily reminder of his faithfulness. Every evening as I walk through that kitchen that was once empty but is now full of noisy women and children, I cannot help but remember that powerful day many years ago when God showed me that same, exact vision to illustrate that it was his plan and not mine. Little did I know then, every one of those women and children would one day represent a breathtaking miracle. God must have smiled to himself in that moment, because he knew that all along.

The incredible view I see when I leave for the day

"For I know the plans I have for you," declares the Lord, "plans to prosper you and not to harm you, plans to give you hope and a future. Then you will call on me and come and pray to me, and I will listen to you. You will seek me and find me when you seek me with all your heart." (Jeremiah 29:11–13)

EPILOGUE

I have already been making a list of things to do when I get to heaven, which I realize is ridiculous. For instance, I plan to fly like a bird, I want an answer to where God came from, and I hope to finally understand why bad things happen to good people.

There is another big item on that list, and I am reminded of it every time someone asks, "Can you believe what has happened at Blue Monarch?" Truth is, I have intentionally tried not to think about it. My fear was that if I really stopped to absorb all the women and children changed and impacted through Blue Monarch, I would start crying and never stop, because it would be so emotionally overwhelming. My response has always been, "I'll wait and think about that when I get to heaven."

This book has forced me to go through that process early. I shed many tears as I reflected on these stories and relived those rich moments and events over the past twenty years. A movie reel has been running nonstop in my head with countless faces stirring feelings of all kinds. There were miracles tucked away in my heart that rose to the surface and took my breath away for the second time.

I realized, however, that many of my tears were because I still felt so unworthy to participate in what has taken place. Truth is, I don't even feel worthy to put a decal of a fish on my car just in case I accidentally flip someone off in traffic someday. This assignment feels like a gift for which there are no words to adequately express how humbled I am to receive it.

A few months before this Blue Monarch journey began, I was resting in the sun on a deck that Clay and I have that overlooks the neighboring state park. Suddenly the realistic head of a wolf appeared right in front of my face, staring at me with menacing eyes, which felt very threatening. The image was so close and so clear, I could see the hollow pupils of the wolf's eyes and the geometric shapes in the golden irises. I stared back, determined not to move, unsure what might happen next. The wolf eventually faded away, leaving me quite puzzled as to the meaning.

In looking back, I believe it was yet another preview into the spiritual battle I was about to enter. And I feel the fact that I did not back off from the wolf is one of the reasons I was given this incredible appointment. God knew Blue Monarch was going to undo the ugly destruction of hundreds, perhaps thousands of families, and the fight would be intense and powerful. So, even with all my faults, many years out of the church, three husbands, and an occasional bad word, he knew I was stubborn enough to stand and never back down.

For most of my life, I avoided eye contact with God and only lived the cover of my Bible from the perspective of an outsider. But this Blue Monarch journey has allowed me to step inside and experience the pages in living color.

I now see scripture that used to sound theoretical as absolute truth that gives us specific instructions and guidance. I know that angels *and* demons are real, because I have seen them and felt their presence. Jesus truly exists, and he's not the stuffy guy I thought he was. He has a great sense of humor and enjoys authentic people who are imperfect. The Holy Spirit is tangible, because he gives me words to say and solutions to problems when there is absolutely no way I should know them. God is undeniably real, because I have seen how he loves and protects his children in a way that is humanly impossible, his hand is in even the smallest details, and he extends grace even when it makes no sense on paper to do so. And miracles are not just something that happened in Bible times. They happen on a daily basis all around us.

When I think back over everything that has transpired since that powerful dream many years ago, I can see that my greatest peace came when I was blindly obedient, and I experienced the most comfort when I had faith to walk on water even though I knew I couldn't. But one thing is very clear: there was no way to have either when I took my eyes off Jesus.

May I never avoid eye contact again.

> *Now glory be to God, who by his mighty power at work within us is able to do far more than we would ever dare to ask or even dream of—infinitely beyond our highest prayers, desires, thoughts, or hopes.* (Ephesians 3:20 TLB)

ACKNOWLEDGMENTS

I would like to thank my father, Bob Lowery, for telling me I could do anything, and my mother, Bobbie Jean Lowery, for worrying that I believed him but supporting me anyway; Mary Susan McConnell, for giving me the nudge I needed more times than I can count; Abiella McConnell, who inspires me from a place in my heart that belongs only to her; and my husband, Clay Binkley, for being such a good sport when I brought home an eight-hundred-pound gorilla named Blue Monarch, which wasn't in the deal. I can't imagine surviving this experience without him.

I also appreciate the amazing team at Blue Monarch that also bleeds blue—and shares in the tears as well as the laughter; Kate Cataldo for absorbing my passion for Blue Monarch, protecting it with a fierce heart, and mimicking everything I do, say, and wear, which is the greatest compliment of all; Jeannie Driver Campbell for partnering with me through this profound journey from the very beginning and demonstrating supernatural strength every single day; and Deanna Lambert, who is the smartest person I know and brilliant at turning my ideas into reality. I am thankful for our small but mighty board that shares big-picture ideas with faith and great stewardship; and for Madeline and Howell Adams, who believed in me when they had no reason to; and for the select families who poured significant resources into our campus, which catapulted us to each new level of growth. And what would we do without all the countless folks who have contributed their time and resources to make Blue Monarch possible? Of course, I must thank Alicia Alexander, who urged me to begin sharing my stories in the form of a blog (even though I strongly resisted), and Holly Crawshaw, who edited them with such care and enthusiasm.

Without the raw courage and fierce determination of the women and children we serve, there would be no stories to tell, so I hope I have honored our Blue Monarch families in the way their journeys have been shared.

Most of all, I am thankful for my heavenly Father, who went down the list and decided to give me a chance despite all the reasons he probably shouldn't have. It was the greatest gift I could have ever imagined, even though I was tempted to return it many times, for which I now apologize.

Post Office Box 1207
Monteagle, Tennessee 37356
(931) 924-8900
info@bluemonarch.org
www.bluemonarch.org